D1205681

# The HERMITAGE

# WESTERN EUROPEAN PAINTING
## 13th to 18th Centuries

# The HERMITAGE

AURORA ART PUBLISHERS · ST PETERSBURG

Introduction by Tatyana Kustodieva

Compiled by

Yekaterina Deriabina, Natalia Gritsai, Liudmila Kagané, Tatyana Kustodieva,
Nikolai Nikulin, Yelizaveta Renne, Clara Semionova, Natalia Serebriannaya,
Irina Sokolova and Svetlana Vsevolozhskaya

Translated from the Russian by Ashkhen Mikoyan
Designed by Irina Luzhina
Edited by Irina Lvova and Svetlana Pavlova

© Aurora Art Publishers, St Petersburg, 1993

Э $\frac{4903020000\text{-}008}{023(01)\text{-}93}$ без объявления

Printed and bound in Russia

ISBN-5-7300-0581-4

This book introduces the reader to the highlights of the Hermitage collection — works by painters of the past, from the thirteenth to the eighteenth century.

Paintings by Old Masters... Giotto and Rembrandt, El Greco and Watteau, Van Eyck and Rubens. Where does the borderline between old and new painting lie? According to tradition, modern history begins with the English Revolution; in the history of painting it is the French Revolution that may be regarded as the beginning of the new era. The innovations introduced into painting in the nineteenth century developed further in the twentieth century.

In 1904, the celebrated Russian poet, Valery Briusov, wrote the poem *Lanterns*, symbolically representing each era in art history by a certain colour or light:

> O centuries like lanterns! How numerous in the gloom,
> Strung out upon the thread of time, in my mind you loom.
> With flames of great diversity, you beguile my sight...
> Some lamps burn clearly, others give a lesser light
> · · · · · · · · · · · · · · · · · · · · · · · · · · · · · · · · · ·
> The Age of Dante is a mysterious glow of ominous gold,
> While in an azure radiance, Leonardo I behold.
>
> (Translated by Paul Williams)

The earliest painting in this book, the *Crucifix* by Ugolino di Tedici, dates from the second half of the thirteenth century, the age of Dante, "the last poet of the Middle Ages and the first poet of the new era". The thirteenth and fourteenth centuries were dominated by the Italian Proto-Renaissance, when culture, although still firmly linked with the past, was already giving birth to new forms that anticipated the great revolution in the history of humanity — the Renaissance. Dante's contemporary, another great Florentine, Giotto, was accordingly the last painter of the medieval period and the first painter of the modern. It is not without reason that he is often referred to as the father of Western European painting. It is from his art that Western European Renaissance painting inherited its interest in reality and its new vision and interpretation of the world. At the same time it was not until the fifteenth century that Giotto's artistic innovations were understood and developed to their fullest potential.

Valery Briusov's image of the age of Dante, as applied to art, is perhaps not completely accurate: the painting of the trecento can hardly be described as "ominous"; "gold", on the other hand, is an epithet which constantly comes to mind by itself with a glance at trecento paintings.

Byzantine icon-painting, whose canons had undergone very little change in the course of almost ten centuries, exerted a great influence upon Western European, particularly Italian, painting. Thirteenth- and fourteenth-century painting was characterized by a schematic representation and a disconnection between the image depicted and the forms existing in objective reality. Almost without exception the background of Byzantine icons was a golden surface which served as a kind of barrier between the artist's world and the real one.

5

The thoughts of Byzantine painters were centred on the celestial and on the Saviour rather than on the real world which was considered sinful, wretched, miserable and base. They wanted their pictures to show man full of sin and trouble, a poor creature whose way through the "dark wood" of life was but an instant followed by the eternity of the other world.

The fourteenth century, the period when Western European culture was at its peak, was marked with the development of Gothic art. But Italy, due to its unique position as the direct heir to the culture of Classical Antiquity, and as the country where capitalism had emerged earlier than elsewhere, never followed the Gothic models as faithfully as France or Germany.

Even though Gothic art was among the sources that inspired Giotto, his novel approach, which placed the viewer in direct contact with paintings, was basically opposed to its underlying principle. In addition, Giotto's works have none of the spirituality which distinguishes Gothic art and is evident in the paintings of many of his contemporaries, for example, Simone Martini of Siena, whose pictures enchant the spectator with their bright colouring, their supple and expressive contours and their lyrical images.

As late as the fifteenth century, during the early Renaissance, many painters were still paying tribute to medieval art. But it was not the conservative trends that determined the character of the period, but the progressive ones — those which reflected the new artistic outlook and perception of the world.

The centre of gravity was shifted, and medieval asceticism was gradually replaced by humanism. Art retained its religious outward appearance, but became secular in content. Nature was from now on the artist's first teacher, and man — the principal criterion of all values. With the growing links between painting and the developing sciences, artists began to master the laws of perspective and to arrive at an anatomically correct representation of the human figure.

In the fifteenth century, the Renaissance spread from Italy to the Netherlands. But unlike Italy, a country with a steady classical foundation and a new humanistic outlook, the Netherlands embraced the Renaissance ideals of man and nature without breaking with the medieval conventional iconography and artistic devices of the past. Netherlandish painters of the time lacked the artistic consistency of the Italian school of the Renaissance and had never had immediate contact with the classical tradition. They were also isolated from the latest scientific achievements since Netherlandish science was less advanced than Italian. Thus, Netherlandish art remained profoundly religious. Netherlandish painting in its development owed much to medieval miniature painting with its minutely careful narrative representation and its concern for verisimilitude in the treatment of space and objects (a quality inspired by the Italian Proto-Renaissance). While the advent of the Renaissance in Italy was marked by a radical denial of former artistic canons, in the Netherlands, by way of contrast, it was an evolutionary process rather than a revolutionary change.

Italian anthropocentrism was completely alien to Netherlandish painters. They treated every manifestation of nature — alive or dead — as equally worthwhile. The Italian artist of the Renaissance can be imagined holding a necklace in his hands adorned with a large diamond pendant that overshadows the rest of the gems in the necklace. For the Netherlandish painter, on the other hand, all the gems in the necklace would be of equal value and beauty.

6

The Netherlandish master minutely described all that surrounded him, and endowed even the homeliest and simplest things with a special vividness and charm. It was this particular charm that two centuries later inspired Dutch painters who also saw beauty and poetry in the homely and the ordinary.

But in certain respects Netherlandish artists were ahead of their Italian contemporaries — first of all, it was their extraordinary development of technical skill that made it possible to render light-and-shade effects as well as the damp atmosphere characteristic of the Low Countries. They also developed oil-painting techniques that were adopted by the Italians only towards the end of the fifteenth century.

One of the first Italian artists to master this new technique was Leonardo da Vinci whose creative work crowned fifteenth-century art and paved the way for that of the sixteenth century.

The Golden Age of the Renaissance was the first two decades of the cinquecento, when it appeared that the desired ideal — the image of the perfect man living in harmony with the beautiful world around him — had been achieved. Looking at the fine pictures by Leonardo, Raphael, Giorgione, the young Michelangelo and Titian it is easy to believe that this actually was so. On the other hand, masterpieces, such as Leonardo's *Mona Lisa*, the *Sistine Madonna* by Raphael, the *Sleeping Venus* by Giorgione, *David* by Michelangelo and the *Sacred and Profane Love* by Titian, were created during a turbulent period of Italian history, dominated by popular uprisings, foreign invasions, the capture of Rome by Charles V in 1527 and the capitulation of the Florentine Republican rebellion in 1530. These political events signified the decline and fall of the Renaissance.

The "azure radiance" of the Italian Renaissance began to dim in the gloom of the Counter-Reformation. The second half of the sixteenth century was a time of confusion and chaos, when several tragic works of art appeared, such as Michelangelo's *Last Judgement* painted near the end of his life, or Titian's *St Sebastian* executed when the artist was 80 years old.

In some European countries the sixteenth century saw both the social restlessness and the flourishing of fine arts.

"The large lamp of Luther", to quote Valery Briusov again, exposed the contradictions that were tearing apart Germany, with her peasant wars and the growing protests against the domination of local princes and the Roman Catholic church. But crucial points in history may give birth to geniuses. Germany could boast a painter of genius, Albrecht Dürer, the founder of the German Renaissance.

The heady tramping of dancing peasants in Dürer's prints is echoed by the lumbering dance of peasants making merry under the gallows in a painting by Pieter Brueghel the Elder, a younger contemporary of Dürer. But while Dürer's art marked the beginning of sixteenth-century German painting, Brueghel's creative work signified the end of the Netherlandish painting of the same period. Brueghel, a philosopher as well as an artist, often approaches the grotesque by juxtaposing the tragic with the comic. His paintings reflect the reality of his time, which was dominated by the Rebellion. The Netherlands split into two separate states — Holland, a free republic, and Flanders, a country still under Spanish control.

The social and political conditions in France at this time were entirely different from those in Italy and Germany, where the lack of centralized power led to political decline and reaction, and in the Netherlands, where the sixteenth century ended with a victorious

7

bourgeois revolution. France was steadily turning into an absolute monarchy. Experts may disagree about the boundaries of the French Renaissance, but the sixteenth century was certainly the period of its flourishing. The most outstanding accomplishment of this period was the Château of Fontainebleau. It became the centre of the Renaissance art in France. For its decoration Francis I commissioned such Italian artists as Fiorentino Rosso, Francesco Primaticcio and Benvenuto Cellini. Leonardo also left Italy at the invitation of the French court and spent the last years of his life there: he died at Cloux, near Amboise, in 1519. The country of classical Gothic art, France was readily adopting Italian Mannerism, whose refinement, sophistication and elaborateness appealed to the aristocracy. Another manifestation of the Renaissance in France was the development of the portrait. It was distinguished by a precision of form, probably inherited from medieval sculpture, and a highly expressive characterization of the model. For all that, however, the depiction still retains much of the rigidity absent in its Italian or even Netherlandish counterparts.

The seventeenth century saw a tremendous advance in the painting of various national schools. It is difficult to say which country took the lead. Each had its own great artists: Italy had Caravaggio and the brothers Carracci, Spain — Zurbarán and Veláz-quez, in Holland there were Hals and Rembrandt, in Flanders — Rubens and Van Dyck, and in France — the brothers Le Nain and Poussin.

In the seventeenth century, a variety of stylistic trends ensured a comprehensive picture of reality with all its complexities and controversies. The Renaissance concept of man as a measure of all things was no longer recognized as the leading principle of art. From now on he was just a small part of the enormous world which lived by its own laws and largely ruled man's life. Therefore, the principal task of an artist was to determine the place of the individual in society and to comprehend the fundamental characteristics of both man and the universe.

The highlight of seventeenth-century Italian art was the work of Caravaggio. His powerful realism both fascinated and shocked his contemporaries. His goal was to make his subject easily recognizable to the viewer: he did not throw upon it the veil of ideal-ization demanded by academic doctrine which attempted to raise reality to the level of art. In order to render volume and depth Caravaggio employed sharp contrasts of light and shade. The homely and prosaic subjects of his pictures challenged the society in which he lived and inspired many seventeenth-century masters who also began to strive towards realism in their paintings. Paintings of such different artists as Rembrandt, Rubens, Velázquez, Ribera and the brothers Le Nain show an obvious debt to Caravaggio.

Concurrently with Caravaggism there developed the academic school of Rome and Bologna headed by the brothers Carracci. In quest of their own artistic system the brothers proclaimed classical (mainly Renaissance) examples as models for imitation. Even though they did not completely denounce painting from life, they believed that an artist should improve upon nature in accordance with the classical canons of beauty. One might imagine that the result of such a theory could only be uninspired, feeble imitation, and to some extent this was the case. At the same time the Carracci family and their numerous followers made several contributions to the development of painting: they were fine monumentalists, they elaborated a highly harmonious and consistent system of peda-gogical principles and, above all, they possessed unquestionable professionalism in the best and loftiest sense of the word.

When examining art history, it is often difficult to draw distinct lines between various tendencies. Thus, Caravaggio's works revealed at times traces of Mannerism, while the head of the academic trend, Annibale Carracci, painted one of the first Italian genre scenes, *The Bean Eaters*. Likewise, the cold academic style, paradoxical as it may seem, eventually gave birth to the pompous Baroque style with its tension, stormy dynamism and contrasts.

Sometimes the seventeenth century as a whole is described as the age of the Baroque. But the artistic phenomena at that time were so varied and multiform that they can hardly be covered by a single stylistic label. Apart from Italy, the Baroque was flourishing in Catholic Flanders, where it found its most brilliant expression in the work of Peter Paul Rubens.

In Rubens's paintings the world — immense and overwhelming in its variety of forms — was presented in perpetual movement; it shone with iridescent colours and glorified the joys of life. It was also a scene of permanent struggle — between nature and man, between man and wild beasts, between good and evil. In the end, the hero is always victorious, triumphing over all ordeals and hazards, and thus Glory crowns Perseus, the saviour of Andromeda, and a wreath of vine leaves adorns the head of Bacchus, and golden wine flows in abundance, for there is thrilling joy in the battle, and the rapture of passions means the rapture of life itself.

Rubens's work encompasses every genre of painting. Other Flemish painters, however, tended to concentrate on one particular genre alone. Thus, the colourful exuberance of life was the main theme in the works of the famous Flemish still-life painter Frans Snyders. His Hermitage shop-pieces defied the accepted terms for still-life painting — neither the French *nature morte*, nor the German *Stilleben* seemed adequate in describing those cornucopian assortments of fish, poultry and dead game. His pictures, showing all the riches of the earth and of the depth of the sea, seem to embody man's dream of abundance. The game, fish, fruit and vegetables excite the spectator's imagination thanks to the exuberance of forms, colours and even — so vivid they are — of scents and tastes.

While Snyders was mainly preoccupied with still life, Van Dyck concentrated on portraiture and Jordaens worked in the field of genre painting. But both Jordaens's scenes, with their vitality and artless gaiety, and Van Dyck's portraits, with their unique precision of characterization, reveal the principal features of the Flemish school — its realism, vividness and spontaneity of perception.

Van Dyck's stay at the court of Charles I and his series of formal portraits made a great impact on English culture, rather than on Flemish; in fact, the flourishing of English portraiture in the eighteenth century would hardly have been possible without the foundations laid by Anthony Van Dyck.

In spite of the common starting point — Netherlandish art of the fifteenth and sixteenth centuries — the Dutch and Flemish schools of painting diverged in the seventeenth century. At the beginning of the century the spirit of the Netherlandish revolution was still alive in both countries. But the bourgeois republican power which was established in Holland led to the purely secular and democratic character of Dutch painting. Being a Protestant country, Holland was not dominated by the dictatorship of the Church to such an extent as Flanders and other Catholic countries. The interior of a Protestant church was simple and had nothing of the lofty splendour of Catholic churches. It was

9

natural therefore that painting received a different orientation — its function most often was to decorate the interior of the burgher's house. Hence the subjects which could interest ordinary people and which were drawn from real life; hence the small size of pictures and, finally, the diversity of genres which catered to the tastes of merchants and sailors. Holland provided its artists with rich and varied material, and Rembrandt's words may be regarded as the creative credo of any Dutch painter: "The sky, the earth, the sea, animals, good and evil people — they are all there for us to paint. Valleys and hills, creeks and trees give enough work to artists. Cities and markets, churches and thousands of natural treasures appeal to us, saying: come, you, who thirst for knowledge, contemplate and reproduce us. In your homeland you will find so many things that will become dear to your heart, so many pleasant and worthy things, that, having perceived them once, you will find that your lives are too short for embodying them all in your art."

The seventeenth century saw the final division of painting into separate genres, and in no other country was that process so apparent and consistent as in Holland, where the differentiation continued even within individual genres. Thus, among landscape painters there were marinists and those who specialized in painting plains, those who preferred winter views or night landscapes; some of the animalists painted only birds, others only domestic animals; some artists favoured church interiors, while others were interested in secular ones. Even among still-life painters there were several "specialities": there were flower and fish painters, and also those who specialized in what have come to be called "breakfast pieces".

Pictures on religious subjects were still occasionally produced, but Biblical scenes were treated in terms of familiar everyday life: for example, in Abraham Bloemaert's canvas *Landscape with the Prophet Elijah*, Elijah finds seclusion in the backyard of a peasant's farm instead of in the wilderness, and in Gabriel Metsu's painting the prodigal son is shown carousing in a brothel.

Dutch artists, conventionally referred to as the "minor Dutchmen", represented one of the most widely spread professions in the country: painters were numerous in those days, and their pictures were sold and bought on equal terms with all other goods; therefore, they had to cater for the tastes of burghers who were their main customers and patrons. Among the "minor Dutchmen" were both well-known artists and mediocre painters, but all of them turned to real life for their subject matter.

It was Rembrandt, however, who attained a deep philosophic perception of the world and depicted its spiritual wealth and beauty, the homely and the elevated, the lyrical and the tragic in life. His art indubitably occupies a place among the greatest achievements of world culture.

The fine collection of Rembrandt's paintings in the Hermitage follows the artist's creative progress from his early portraits, where a desire to render characteristic features of the model is combined with a typically Dutch emphasis on objects, to the mature ones, where everything — composition, light and colour — serves the principal aim of revealing the subtleties of the human soul: from the *Danaë*, which shows a human being at the sublime moment of fulfilling an innermost desire, to the *Return of the Prodigal Son*, where all expressive means, including light and reddish-brown colour scheme, serve to convey the depth of human suffering.

Second to Rembrandt in Dutch painting was Frans Hals. A great innovator in the field of portraiture, Hals cast off the existing canons and introduced into painting hitherto

10

unknown ease and freedom. The originality of Hals's manner, his bold and unrestrained stroke and his novel artistic vision were far ahead of his time.

The seventeenth century is often referred to as the Golden Age of Spanish culture. Spanish painting particularly flourished at the time when the claims of the Spanish monarchy to world supremacy proved futile. Although the Church's influence in Spain was stronger than elsewhere in Europe, the national spirit retained its inexorable vitality in art characterized by its realistic orientation and ultimate truthfulness. Ribera's dramatic force, Zurbarán's austere simplicity, Murillo's lyrical images, and, as the crowning glory of the whole, Velázquez's genius, together formed the Spanish artistic scene in the seventeenth century.

Velázquez began as a genre painter. He found his models among the people of Seville and painted them at their daily work. Later in his career he became Court Painter to Philip IV and, apart from portraits of the royal family and of the court dwarfs and jesters, he also painted pictures on historical and mythological subjects. But whatever the subject matter, Velázquez always aimed at absolute truth in his works. The integrity of his artistic outlook, the beauty of his palette and his exceptional treatment of light and air ensured Velázquez's influence upon many generations of artists, even including the French Impressionists.

The consolidation of the French absolute monarchy, which had begun in the sixteenth century, culminated in the next century in the reign of Louis XIV. The royal power required a splendid setting, and the official taste for exuberance and grandeur found expression in the Baroque style. Alongside with the latter, however, a number of other artistic styles developed in France.

In fact, the age of Corneille and Racine found its most representative manifestation in Classicism, the style based on the art of Classical Antiquity and, to a certain extent, of the Renaissance. An art of lofty passions expressed through simple and austere media, Classicism was most fully displayed in the works of Nicolas Poussin. The crystal clarity of Poussin's canvases conveyed the ideas of civic duty, the priority of reason over feeling and a strict self-control. His mythological scenes, landscapes and Biblical episodes possessed a high ethical meaning and at the same time complied with the strict canons of Classicism.

Similar tendencies in landscape painting were developed by Claude Lorrain (Claude Gellée) whose idealized views, full of harmony and perfection, reveal none the less the artist's concrete observations.

The third major trend of seventeenth-century French art was the realism of the so-called *peintres de la réalité*, of which the most notable was Georges de La Tour. He, as well as other artists of this trend, was either directly or indirectly influenced by Caravaggio's art. La Tour concentrated mainly on religious subjects which he transformed into scenes of everyday life, endowing them with sincerity and warmth. The brothers Le Nain — Antoine, Louis and Mathieu (the latter only at the early stages of his career) — were the first French painters to find their subjects in real contemporary life and to introduce peasant scenes into the repertory of genres.

The eighteenth century in France began with the last decades of the long reign of Louis XIV (1643—1715) and ended with the first year of Napoleon's rule as First Consul. "Two tiny stars — the age of vain marquises", was what Valery Briusov wrote about the eighteenth century, but, in fact, those "vain marquises" were but an insignificant trifle compared with the grandiose events of that century. It began when impoverished

11

France was still extolling *le roi soleil* and ended with the storming of the Bastille, that formidable symbol of French absolutism, on July 14th, 1789, when the words "Liberté, Egalité, Fraternité" became the slogans of the day. At the close of the century France was still a republic, but in a few years' time the First Consul declared himself Emperor and the days of the French Republic were over.

The eighteenth century in France was the age of the Enlightenment, described by the nineteenth-century Russian critic Vissarion Belinsky as "the age of negation": the Encyclopaedists Voltaire, Diderot, Montesquieu and Rousseau condemned the declining feudal system and the domination of the Church. Their incisive criticism, however, eventually led to a new positive outlook on the world in general and on the role of art in particular.

In painting, the eighteenth century was opened by Jean-Antoine Watteau. His pictures were impossible to pigeonhole according to the classes of painting that the Academy recognized and accepted. That is why he was admitted to the Academy under the title of *peintre de fêtes galantes*, which was specially invented for him. This seemed the only adequate description of a painter whose poetic scenes were inhabited by exquisite ladies and gentlemen making music, dancing and daydreaming under trees or on palace terraces. It was an imaginative, theatrical world without any familiar action, plot or setting. Watteau's paintings fascinated the spectators with their vagueness and melancholic grace. Nobody had ever dressed like Watteau's ladies, in fact the reverse is true — his paintings started a new fashion in dress.

A lonely, unsociable and destitute man, Watteau had no pupils (apart from Pater). His influence, however, was great enough for art historians to refer to the "school of Watteau". His art paved the way for the exquisite and refined style of Rococo, though Watteau himself was not a Rococo painter. The art of aristocracy, capricious and whimsical, Rococo glorified the pleasures of life and the retreat into the world of intimacy. The words traditionally ascribed to Louis XV, "après nous le déluge", could also be regarded as an epigraph to the art created for the "vain marquises". The favourite painter of Marquise de Pompadour, François Boucher, flooded the noblemen's mansions with innumerable nymphs and cupids, shepherds and shepherdesses. Boucher's paintings, with their pretentious blue-and-pink colouring (a typically Rococo combination) and their hints of voluptuousness, looked insincere and artificial.

The advocates of "righteous", moralizing and didactic art severely criticized Boucher and Rococo painting as a whole. "His elegance, affectation, romantic gallantry," Diderot wrote, "his coquetry, taste, variety, his lustre, rouged bodies and libertinism must delight dandies, frivolous women and young men of fashion, in short, the throng of those who are alien to genuine taste, truth, the right notions and austerity." The Encyclopaedists found their ideal in the art of the "third estate" which was later to play a decisive role in the French Revolution. Among its most notable exponents were Chardin and Greuze. They represented that "righteous" painting which instructed people and extolled civic and family virtues, depicting subjects from the life of the bourgeoisie and not of the aristocracy.

Diderot always passionately and persistently defended his point of view and, perhaps for this reason, he failed to detect Greuze's sentimentality and his inner affinity with the Rococo style. In 1763, when Greuze exhibited his *Paralytic* at the Salon, Diderot expressed his ardent admiration: "This painting is good, very good, and I pity those who will remain unmoved by it!" Two years later, the Russian Ambassador to France and a connoisseur of art Prince Golitsyn bought the *Paralytic* on Diderot's recommendation for the newly-founded Hermitage picture gallery in St Petersburg.

The history of art collecting in Russia goes back to the age of Peter the Great, a period of drastic changes and innovations. At that time the first Russian museum, the *Kunstkammer*, was founded. In addition, a small collection of paintings was housed in the Palace of Monplaisir in Peterhof, the Tsar's summer residence. During his trips abroad, Peter got acquainted with European art, which was completely alien to Russians since Russian painting before Peter's time had been exclusively confined to icon-painting.

Peter's ambition was to keep pace with Western Europe in all aspects of life, and this included art collecting. Above all he was a passionate collector of Dutch art, hence the enormous collection of Dutch painting in the present-day Hermitage.

Catherine the Great regarded art collecting as a matter of state policy aimed at consolidating the country's authority and international prestige. In 1764 she commissioned the building of a special pavilion to house a collection of 225 pictures bought from Gotzkowsky, a Berlin merchant. The pavilion was named the Hermitage, and the museum originally set up as the court picture gallery still retains this name.

The purchase of pictures from Gotzkowsky was a wise political move on Catherine's part. First, Russia began accumulating a representative art collection, similar to those already assembled at many European courts, and second, Catherine demonstrated the reliability of her treasury. Gotzkowsky had collected these paintings for Friedrich II, but the King of Prussia's financial difficulties prevented him from buying them. And thus Russia showed that she could do something that Prussia could not. From then on the Hermitage regularly purchased works of art, usually not individual pieces, but entire collections, and famous ones at that.

Catherine II did not rely upon her own artistic taste — she admitted her total ignorance in music and painting, and her sole passion was for carved gems. She therefore enlisted the assistance of Diderot, Baron Grimm and Prince Golitsyn, the ambassador to Paris and later to The Hague. She also corresponded with Voltaire and invited the French sculptor Falconet to work in St Petersburg. Incidentally, Diderot, although eventually enthusiastic about Catherine's art collecting, was originally rather sceptical about her project. "It is impossible," he wrote, "that Russia could ever collect an amount of paintings sufficient for developing a genuine taste for art." Meanwhile Russia went on collecting, and the amount of pictures was growing rapidly.

Among the most fortunate acquisitions made in the late eighteenth century was *The Return of the Prodigal Son* by Rembrandt. Among the most notable purchased collections were those of Count Heinrich von Brühl (1769), Prime Minister under Augustus III, King of Poland and Elector of Saxony, of François Tronchin of Geneva (1770) and, in particular, of the famous French collector Pierre Crozat (1772). The latter collection included such masterpieces as *Judith* by Giorgione, *The Holy Family* by Raphael, *The Nativity of St John the Baptist* by Tintoretto and others.

Diderot's scepticism, therefore, proved unfounded. In 1790, Catherine II wrote to Grimm: "My museum in the Hermitage consists, not counting the pictures and Raphael's loggias, of 38,000 books, four rooms filled with books and prints, 10,000 carved gems,

13

some 10,000 drawings and a section of natural history specimens taking up two large rooms." The Hermitage collection of paintings at that time included about 3,000 items. Apart from the royal collection, a number of private ones were established in the eighteenth century. After the October Revolution of 1917, many of these became part of the Hermitage depository.

The nineteenth century, particularly its first half, saw a further growth of the Hermitage collections. The Hermitage itself was turned into a public museum (1854). Among the best items acquired in the nineteenth century was a group of paintings from Malmaison, Empress Josephine's gallery, and from the English banker Coesvelt collection.

In 1864, the Duke of Litta offered his collection to the management of the Hermitage. Among the paintings selected by S. Gedeonov, Director of the Hermitage of the time, from the Duke's Milan collection was Leonardo da Vinci's *Madonna and Child*, now commonly known as *The Litta Madonna*.

Several years later Gedeonov succeeded in negotiating with Count Conestabile the purchase of one of the best early works by Raphael, *Madonna with the Book* (*The Conestabile Madonna*). For centuries the Conestabile family and the city of Perugia had prided themselves on their possession of that picture.

In the middle of the last century, an extension was built onto the eighteenth-century buildings of the Old and the Small Hermitages. It was named the New Hermitage and was designed not as a palace pavilion, but as a museum whose interiors were suited for the best possible display of the collections. The picture gallery was allocated rooms on the first floor.

Although the Museum was becoming more and more accessible to the public (first to a limited circle of people outside the court and then to the public at large), it still remained an extension of the Imperial residence, the Winter Palace.

Much was done for "the depository of human genius" by the Russian art-lovers. Several large private collections were bequeathed to the Hermitage. In 1911, the Museum acquired from the Stroganov collection such masterpieces as the *Madonna* from *The Annunciation* diptych by Simone Martini and the reliquary by Fra Angelico. A notable contribution to the English section was a group of first-class eighteenth-century portraits from the Khitrovo collection (received from 1912 to 1916). The celebrated Russian geographer Semionov-Tien-Shansky sold his pictures to the Hermitage at half the price offered to him by some foreign art-dealers. He had been collecting pictures by Flemish and Dutch masters for almost half a century, giving preference to those artists whose creative work had no or little representation in the Hermitage. The Museum purchased his collection in 1910 on the condition that it would remain with the owner until his death. In 1914, when Semionov-Tien-Shansky died, the collection was transferred to the Hermitage. A great event in the Russian cultural life was the purchase in the same year of Leonardo's *Madonna and Child* (*The Benois Madonna*). "It is impossible to remain indifferent to the display of patriotic feeling on the part of the owner, M. A. Benois, which inspired her to sacrifice part of the sale price of the painting for the sake of keeping it in Russia," commented a St Petersburg art magazine. *The Benois Madonna* was the last major acquisition before the October Revolution of 1917.

A new stage of the Museum's development began immediately after the Revolution. In the first days of the Soviet Republic, large private collections were nationalized, and the Hermitage became state property. The nationalization of major art collections became

14

an important source of new additions to the Museum. Among them were the collections which had belonged to such eminent art collectors among the Russian titled aristocracy as Yusupov, Shuvalov, Stroganov, Sheremetev and others.

It is sometimes difficult to account for artistic tastes or blind-spots of a particular epoch. Thus, up to the early twentieth century the Hermitage possessed virtually no examples of early Italian painting of the thirteenth and fourteenth centuries, and the fifteenth century was represented only by a few pictures. The addition in the 1920s of the Stroganov collection to the stocks of the Museum was therefore particularly important: the Stroganovs were among the few Russian connoisseurs of art who had been systematically collecting pre-Renaissance Italian painting as early as the second half of the nineteenth century.

Thus, during 229 years of its existence the Hermitage was transformed from a court collection into one of the most famous treasure-houses of world art. Today it is ever developing and expanding. The most valuable acquisitions since 1917 have been a two-sided icon signed by Antonio da Firenze, *The Toilet of Bathsheba* by Pieter Lastman (Rembrandt's teacher), the *Landscape with Bathers* — a joint work by two Dutch painters, Jan Both and Cornelius van Poelenburgh, the *Night Fire* by Claude Vernet, the *Penitent Magdalene* by Giampetrino and several paintings by Adriaen van Ostade and David Teniers. The research staff of the Museum carefully study each new item in the collection. The results of this research work are regularly published in special periodicals and described in the Hermitage catalogues. An interesting example is the recent attribution of *The Adoration of the Magi* to Pietro Negroni of Naples. The canvas was transferred from the National Museum Reserve (an organization responsible for the preservation of works of art) in 1924 and for a long time was believed to be a work by an anonymous sixteenth-century artist from Ferrara. The authorship of many other paintings has also been established (Pietro Dandini's *The Holy Family*, Massimo Stanzione's *Cleopatra*, and *The Dead Christ* by Lorenzo Lotto). The restoration and subsequent study of the *Mourning of Christ*, previously ascribed to the Spanish school, have enabled the experts to attribute it to Jacques Bellange, an early seventeenth-century French follower of Caravaggio, whose extant paintings of unquestionable authenticity are very few. *The Allegoric Scene* by a seventeenth-century German artist turned out to be the work of Joachim von Sandrart based on Aesop's fable *A Middle-aged Man and His Two Mistresses* — a subject unique in world painting.

The times when the Museum was a stationary and self-contained body are past. Its present activities keep pace with the dynamic life of the present century. The Hermitage regularly organizes exhibitions both at the Museum itself and outside its walls, at home and abroad. The anniversaries of many great artists — Rembrandt, Watteau, Caravaggio, Rubens, Jordaens, Veronese and others — were celebrated by the Museum with temporary exhibitions of their works, sometimes accompanied by a display of minor arts of the period.

Loan exhibitions from the Hermitage, both of individual masterpieces and large thematic collections, have received a warm welcome in different parts of the world — in Western Europe, America, Canada, Japan, Australia and elsewhere.

A vivid example of the Museum's vast exhibition activities is its contribution of 25 paintings to the exhibition "Painting by Old Masters from Soviet Museums" held in the 1980s in Sydney and Melbourne. Another example is the exchange of loan exhibitions

15

between the Hermitage and the museums of Madrid and Vienna. The Spanish public was able to see a collection of Dutch and Spanish seventeenth-century paintings from the Hermitage, among them the *Luncheon* and *Count-Duke of Olivares* by Velázquez, *The Adolescence of the Virgin* by Zurbarán, the *Holy Family* by Murillo, *Flora* and two portraits by Rembrandt. Citizens of Vienna were able to admire a collection of Western European paintings of the seventeenth century which included such fine works as *David and Uriah* by Rembrandt, the *Youth with a Lute* by Caravaggio and Van Dyck's *Self-portrait*.

Sending loan exhibitions from the Hermitage to Japan has become a tradition. Art-lovers in Tokyo, Osaka and other cities have paid tribute to works by Rembrandt, paintings and drawings by Flemish and Dutch masters.

The collections of the Hermitage embrace an infinite variety of works of art, but its picture gallery still remains the most notable and comprehensive section of the Museum. The creative potential of human genius manifests itself in different spheres of artistic activity. Painting can be as lyrical as poetry, as emotional as music and as expressive in its narrative aspect as drama or fiction.

The Hermitage gives its visitors a unique opportunity to turn into enchanted wanderers in the magic world of painting.

> With flames of great diversity, you beguile my sight...
> Some lamps burn clearly, others give a lesser light
> Sparkling, multicoloured, in the garden full of wonder,
> In which enchanted I now wander.

# ITALY

Ugolino di Tedici
Simone Martini
Niccolo di Pietro Gerini
Fra Beato Angelico da Fiesole
Gandolfino da Roreto
Bernardino Fungai
Filippino Lippi
Antonio da Firenze
Raphael
Cesare da Sesto
Leonardo da Vinci
Bernardino Luini
Francesco Francia
Perugino
Correggio
Cima da Conegliano
Giorgione
Lorenzo Lotto
Pontormo
Titian
Paolo Veronese
Francesco Primaticcio
Giovanni Battista Naldini
Caravaggio
Annibale Carracci

Agostino Carracci
Domenico Fetti
Alessandro Allori
Antonio Maria Vassallo
Bernardo Strozzi
Salvator Rosa
Giovanni Benedetto Castiglione
Michelangelo da Campidoglio
Francesco Maltese
Carlo Maratti
Giuseppe Maria Crespi
Gaspare Vanvitelli
Alessandro Magnasco
Clemente Spera
Michele Marieschi
Pietro Tempesta
Carlo Bonaria
Giovanni Battista Tiepolo
Pompeo Girolamo Batoni
Francesco Guardi

**1. UGOLINO DI TEDICI.** Active 1260—70
**CRUCIFIX.** *C.* 1270. Tempera on panel. 90×62*. *Transferred in 1926 from the Stroganov Palace Museum, Leningrad.*

**2. SIMONE MARTINI.** *C.* 1284—1344
**MADONNA FROM "THE ANNUNCIATION" DIPTYCH.** After 1333. Tempera on panel. 30.5×21.5. *Acquired in 1911 from the Stroganov collection, Rome, according to the owner's will.*

**3. NICCOLO DI PIETRO GERINI.** Mentioned between 1368 and 1415
**THE CRUCIFIXION WITH THE VIRGIN MARY AND ST JOHN.** 1390s. Tempera on panel. 85.5✕52.7 (103✕57.7 in the
Gothic frame). *Transferred in 1926 from the Stroganov Palace Museum, Leningrad; before that in the Stroganov collection,*
*St Petersburg (1855 bought by P. Stroganov from Trois in Rome).*

**4. FRA BEATO ANGELICO DA FIESOLE (GUIDO DI PIETRO).** *C.* 1400—1455
**MADONNA AND CHILD WITH STS DOMINIC AND THOMAS AQUINAS.** Early 1430s. Fresco. 196×187. *Purchased in 1883 from the artists Alessandro Mazzanti and Cosimo Conti, Florence.*

**5, 6. GANDOLFINO DA RORETO (GANDOLFINO D'ASTI).** Mentioned between 1493 and 1510
**THE NATIVITY OF CHRIST.** Late 1490s—early 1500s. Oil on canvas (transferred from panel). 213×102. *Transferred in 1926 from the Stroganov Palace Museum, Leningrad.*

**8. FILIPPINO LIPPI.** C. 1457—1504
THE ANNUNCIATION. Between 1495 and 1500. Tempera on panel. 35×50.5. *Transferred in 1922 from the Stroganov Palace Museum, Petrograd.*

**9. ANTONIO DA FIRENZE.** Active second half of the 15th century
**MADONNA AND CHILD WITH SAINTS** (obverse of the double-sided icon). Tempera on panel. 151.5×84.5. *Acquired in 1936 through the Leningrad Purchasing Commission; before that in the Botkin collection, Petrograd.*

**10. RAPHAEL (RAFFAELLO SANTI or SANZIO).** 1483—1520
**THE CONESTABILE MADONNA.** C. 1504. Tempera on canvas (transferred from panel). 17.5×18 (the composition is painted within a circle). *Transferred in 1880 from the Winter Palace, St Petersburg; 1871 purchased from the Conestabile collection, Perugia.*

## 11. CESARE DA SESTO. 1477—1523
**THE HOLY FAMILY WITH ST CATHERINE.** *C.* 1520. Oil on canvas (transferred from panel). 89×71. *Acquired in 1769.*

**12. LEONARDO DA VINCI.** 1452—1519
**MADONNA AND CHILD (THE LITTA MADONNA).** 1490—91. Tempera on canvas (transferred from panel). 42 × 33.
*Purchased in 1865 from the Litta collection, Milan.*

**ST SEBASTIAN.** Oil and tempera on canvas (transferred from panel). 196✕106. *Purchased in 1860 from the antiquary Maureau, Paris.*

**14. FRANCESCO FRANCIA.** *C.* 1450—1517
**MADONNA AND CHILD WITH ST LAWRENCE, ST JEROME AND ANGELS.** 1500. Oil on canvas (transferred from panel). 193✕151. *Purchased in 1843 from the Ercolani collection.*

**15. PERUGINO (PIETRO VANNUCCI).** *C.* 1450—1523
**ST SEBASTIAN.** 1493—94. Oil and tempera on panel. 53.5×39.5. *Purchased in 1910 from the Marquise Campanari collection, Rome; before that in the Volkonsky collection, Rome.*

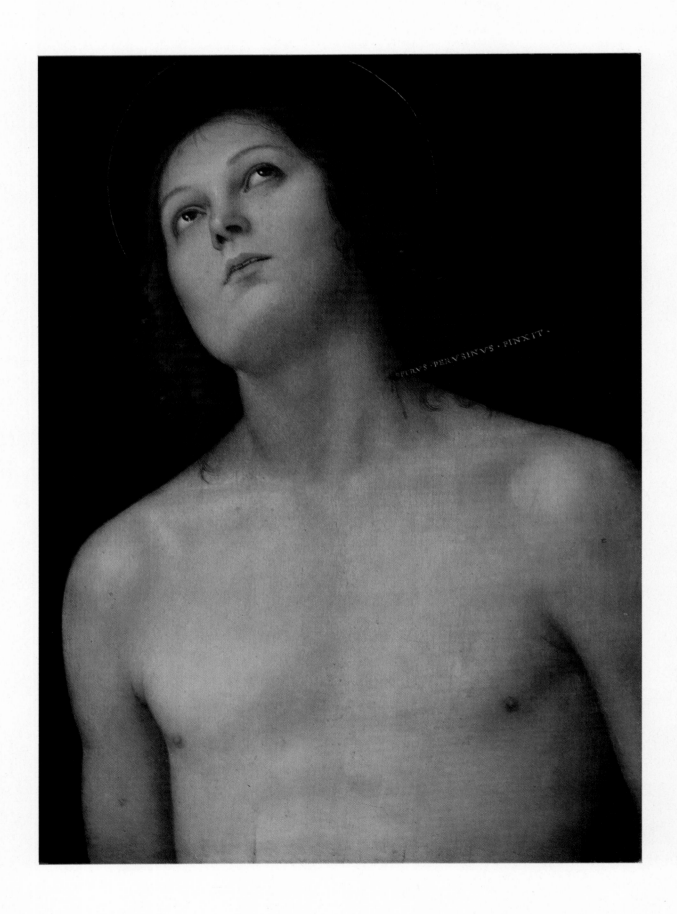

**16. CORREGGIO (ANTONIO ALLEGRI).** 1489—1534
**PORTRAIT OF A LADY.** 1518—19. Oil on canvas. 103×87.5. *Transferred in 1925 from the Yusupov Palace Museum, Leningrad.*

**17. CIMA DA CONEGLIANO (GIOVANNI BATTISTA CIMA).** 1459—1517/18
**THE ANNUNCIATION.** 1495. Oil and tempera on canvas (transferred from panel). 136.5×107. *Transferred in 1886 from the Golitsyn Museum, Moscow.*

**18. GIORGIONE (GIORGIO DA CASTELFRANCO).** C. 1478—1510
**JUDITH.** C. 1504. Oil on canvas (transferred from panel). 144×66,5, *Purchased in 1772 from the Crozat collection, Paris.*

**19. LORENZO LOTTO.** C. 1480—1556
**PORTRAIT OF A MARRIED COUPLE.** 1523—25. Oil on canvas. 96✕116. *Acquired between 1773 and 1785; early 19th century — 1924 Gatchina Palace, near St Petersburg; 1924 transferred back to the Hermitage.*

**20. PONTORMO (JACOPO CARRUCCI).** 1494—1557
**MADONNA AND CHILD WITH ST JOSEPH AND JOHN THE BAPTIST.** 1520s. Oil on canvas (transferred from panel).
120×98.5. *Transferred in 1923 from the National Museum Reserve, Petrograd; before that in the Mordvinova collection.*

**21. TITIAN (TIZIANO VECELLIO).** 1485/90—1576
**ST SEBASTIAN.** Oil on canvas. 210×115. *Purchased in 1850 from the Barbarigo collection, Venice.*

**22. PAOLO VERONESE (PAOLO CALIARI).** 1528—1588
**THE LAMENTATION.** Between 1576 and 1582. Oil on canvas. 147✕111.5. *Purchased in 1772 from the Crozat collection, Paris.*

**23. FRANCESCO PRIMATICCIO.** 1504—1570
**THE HOLY FAMILY WITH ST ELIZABETH AND JOHN THE BAPTIST.** Oil on slate. 43.5×31. *Purchased in 1772 from the Crozat collection, Paris.*

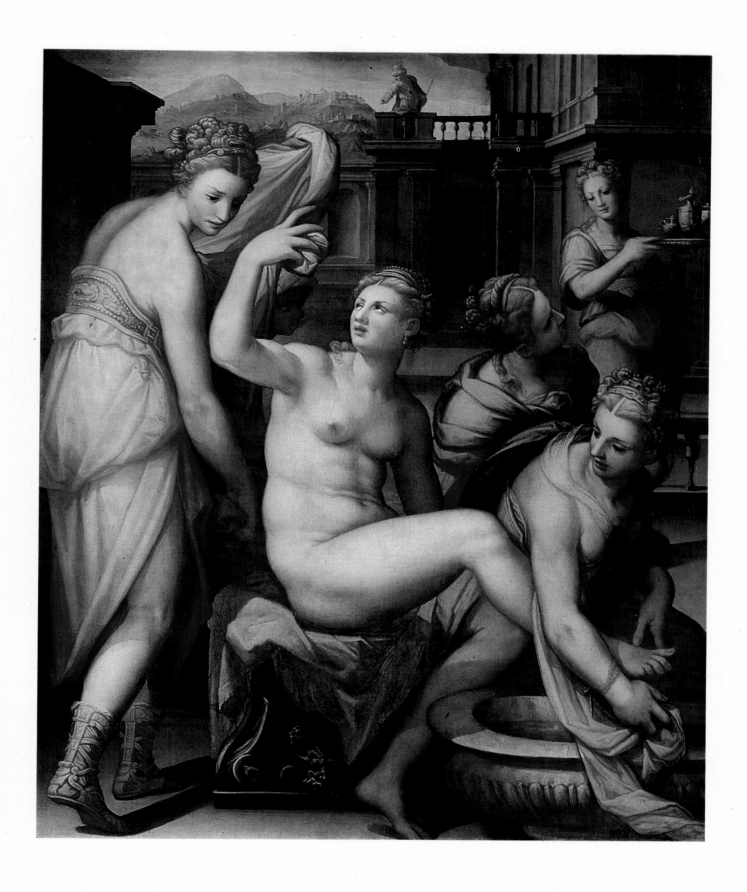

**24. GIOVANNI BATTISTA NALDINI.** 1537—1591
**BATHSHEBA BATHING.** Mid-1570s. Oil on canvas (transferred from panel). 182×150. *Purchased in 1825 in St Petersburg; before that in the Pecori collection, Florence.*

**25, 26. MICHELANGELO MERISI DA CARAVAGGIO.** 1571—1610

**YOUTH WITH A LUTE.** *C. 1596. Oil on canvas. 94×119. Acquired in 1808 (purchased through Vivant-Denon from the Giustiniani collection intended for sale in Paris).*

**28. AGOSTINO CARRACCI.** 1557—1602
**THE LAMENTATION.** 1586 (?). Oil on canvas. 191✕156. *Purchased in 1779 from the Walpole collection, Houghton Hall, England.*

**29.** **DOMENICO FETTI.** 1589—1623
**PORTRAIT OF AN ACTOR.** 1623 (?). Oil on canvas. 105.5×81. *Purchased in 1772 from the Crozat collection, Paris; before that in the collection of Cardinal Mazarin, Paris.*

**30. ALESSANDRO ALLORI.** 1535—1607
**ALLEGORY OF THE CHURCH.** Oil on canvas. 131×115. *Purchased in 1834 from the collection of Paese de la Cadeña, Spanish Ambassador to St Petersburg; until 1931 Catherine Palace, Tsarskoye Selo, near St Petersburg; 1931 transferred back to the Hermitage.*

**31. ANTONIO MARIA VASSALLO.** Born *c.* 1620 (?)
**THE CHILDHOOD OF KING CYRUS.** Oil on canvas. 74.5×110. *Purchased in 1779 from the Walpole collection, Houghton Hall, England.*

**32. BERNARDO STROZZI (IL PRETE GENOVESE).** 1581—1644
**THE HEALING OF TOBIT.** Early 1630s. Oil on canvas. 158×223.5. *Purchased in 1772 from the Crozat collection, Paris.*

**33. SALVATOR ROSA.** 1615—1673
**DEMOCRITUS AND PROTAGORAS.** Early 1660s. Oil on canvas. 185×128. *Purchased in 1779 from the Walpole collection, Houghton Hall, England.*

**34. GIOVANNI BENEDETTO CASTIGLIONE, called IL GRECHETTO.** *C.* 1610—1665
**SATYRS BRINGING GIFTS.** Oil on copper. 52× 67.5. *Purchased in 1772 from the Crozat collection, Paris; 19th century Catherine Palace, Tsarskoye Selo, near St Petersburg; 1920 transferred back to the Hermitage.*

**35. MICHELANGELO DA CAMPIDOGLIO (MICHELANGELO DI PACE; MICHELE PALACE).** 1610—1670
**STILL LIFE WITH GRAPES.** Oil on canvas. 98× 134. *Purchased in 1779 from the Walpole collection, Houghton Hall, England; 19th and early 20th centuries Gatchina Palace, near St Petersburg; 1926 transferred back to the Hermitage.*

**36. FRANCESCO MALTESE (FIERAVINO).** Active in Rome between 1650 and 1680
**STILL LIFE WITH AN ORIENTAL CARPET.** Oil on canvas. 97× 132. *Acquired in 1784 or 1785; 1822—1927 Great Palace, Peterhof, near St Petersburg; 1927 transferred back to the Hermitage.*

**38. GIUSEPPE MARIA CRESPI.** 1665—1747
**SELF-PORTRAIT.** *C.* 1700. Oil on canvas. 60.5 × 50 (oval). *Purchased in 1783 from the Baudouin collection, Paris.*

**39. GASPARE VANVITELLI (GASPAR ADRIAENS VAN WITTEL).** 1653—1736
**A VIEW OF ROME.** 1686. Oil on canvas. 33×72. *Purchased in 1772 from the Crozat collection, Paris; 19th century Gatchina Palace, near St Petersburg; 1920 transferred back to the Hermitage.*

**40. ALESSANDRO MAGNASCO.** 1667—1749
**CLEMENTE SPERA.** Active late 17th and early 18th centuries
**THE BANDITS' BIVOUAC.** 1710s. Oil on canvas. 112×162. *Transferred in 1922 from the Museum of the Academy of Arts, Petrograd.*

**41. MICHELE MARIESCHI.** 1696—1743
**SEASIDE VIEW.** Oil on canvas. 103×145. *Transferred in 1930 from the Museum of the City History, Leningrad.*

**42. PIETRO TEMPESTA (PIETER MULIER).** 1637—1701
**SHIPS IN A ROUGH SEA.** C. 1700. Oil on canvas. 100.5×146.5. *Acquired between 1774 and 1783.*

**43. CARLO BONARIA (BONAVIA).** Active in Naples in the mid-18th century
**TEMPLE OF VENUS IN BAIA.** 1758. Oil on canvas. 78×149. *Purchased in 1970 from M. Rumiantsev, Leningrad.*

**44. GIOVANNI BATTISTA TIEPOLO.** 1696—1770
**MAECENAS INTRODUCING THE LIBERAL ARTS TO THE EMPEROR AUGUSTUS.** 1743. Oil on canvas. 69.5×89.
*Purchased in 1769 from the Brühl collection, Dresden; 19th century Gatchina Palace, near St Petersburg; 1882 transferred back to the Hermitage.*

**45. POMPEO GIROLAMO BATONI.** 1708—1787
**LASCIVIOUSNESS.** 1747. Oil on canvas. 138×100. *Transferred in 1922 from the Museum of the Academy of Arts, Petrograd.*

**46. FRANCESCO GUARDI.** 1712—1793
**LANDSCAPE.** Late 1770s—early 1780s. Oil on canvas. 120×152. *Transferred in 1928 from the Gatchina Palace Museum, near Leningrad.*

# THE NETHERLANDS

Rogier van der Weyden
Robert Campin
Hugo van der Goes
Gerard David
Maerten van Heemskerck
Lucas van Leyden
Jan Provost

Jan Gossaert
Master of the Female Half-lengths
Herri met de Bles
Pieter Brueghel the Younger
Frans Pourbus the Elder

**47. ROGIER VAN DER WEYDEN.** *C.* 1399—1464
**ST LUKE DRAWING A PORTRAIT OF THE VIRGIN.** Oil on canvas (transferred from panel). 102.5×108.5. *In the early 19th century, the painting was kept in a monastery in Spain. In 1813, cut into two parts, it was smuggled out of Spain. The right-hand part of the panel (with St Luke) entered the Hermitage in 1850 from the collection of William II of the Netherlands (The Hague). In 1883, the left-hand part (with the Virgin and Child) was purchased from Baron de Beurnonville in Paris (through Antoine Baer, who brought it to St Petersburg). In 1884, the two parts of the painting were transferred onto canvas and then joined into a complete picture.*

**48, 49. ROBERT CAMPIN (MASTER OF FLÉMALLE).** *C.* 1380—1444
**THE TRINITY. THE VIRGIN AND CHILD BY THE FIRESIDE** (diptych). Oil on panel. 34.3✕24.5 (each panel).
*Bequeathed in 1845 by D. Tatishchev, St Petersburg.*

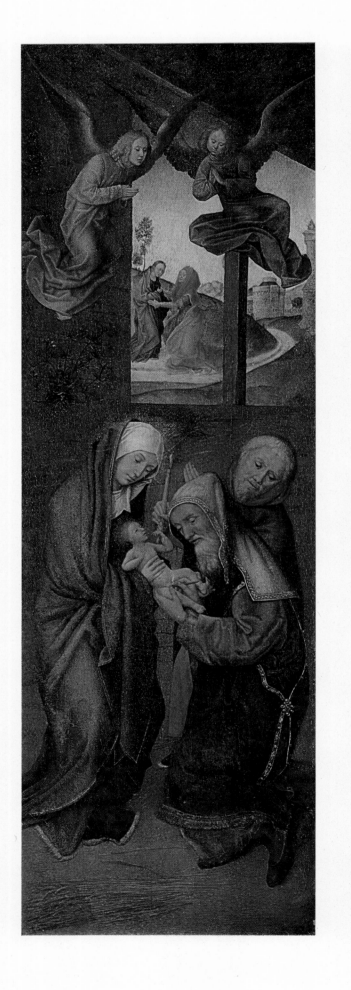
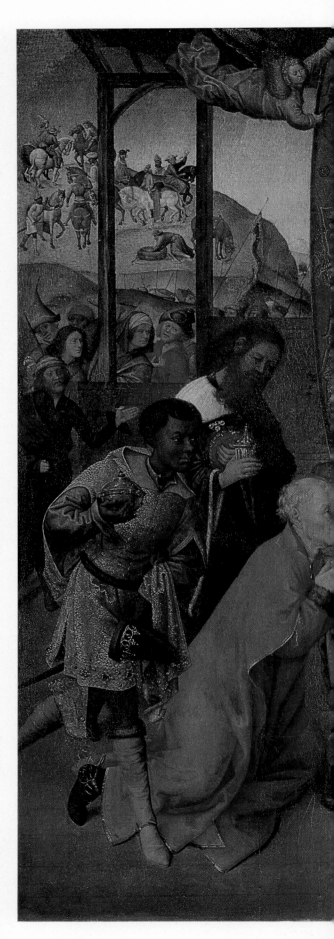

**50—52. HUGO VAN DER GOES.** *C.* 1440—1482
**THE ADORATION OF THE MAGI** (triptych). Oil on canvas (transferred from panel). 96.3×77.5 (central panel);
96.2×31.7 (each wing). *Acquired before 1810.*

**53, 54. GERARD DAVID.** 1460—1523
**THE VIRGIN EMBRACING THE DEAD CHRIST.** Oil on panel. 16.2✕11.4 (centrepiece, top rounded); 36.3✕44.5 (together with the flower surround). *Acquired before 1797.*

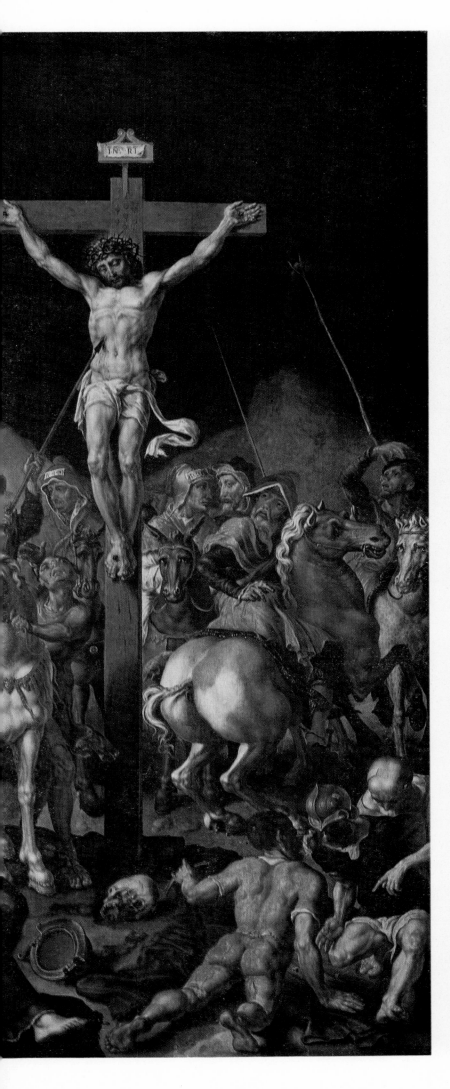

**55—58. MAERTEN VAN HEEMSKERCK. 1498—1574**
CALVARY (triptych). After 1543. Oil on canvas. 100.7×58.3 (centrepiece transferred from panel). Oil on panel, 100.7×28 (each wing). *Purchased in 1811 in Paris through Baron Vivant-Denon.*

**59—61. LUCAS VAN LEYDEN.** 1489/94—1533
**THE HEALING OF THE BLIND MAN OF JERICHO** (triptych). 1531. **59, 60.** Triptych closed. **61.** Triptych open. Oil on canvas (transferred from panel). 115.7×150.3 (central panel with wings); 89×33.5 (outside of the wings with the figures of heralds). *Purchased in 1772 from the Crozat collection, Paris.*

**62. JAN PROVOST.** *C.* 1465—1529
**THE VIRGIN MARY AS QUEEN OF HEAVEN.** 1524. Oil on canvas (transferred from panel). 203✕151 (with a trefoil top).
*Purchased in 1850 from the collection of William II of the Netherlands, The Hague.*

**63. JAN GOSSAERT,** called **MABUSE.** C. 1478—c. 1532
**THE DESCENT FROM THE CROSS.** 1521. Oil on canvas (transferred from panel). 141×106.5 *Acquired in 1850 from
the collection of William II of the Netherlands, The Hague.*

**64. MASTER OF THE FEMALE HALF-LENGTHS.** Active first half of the 16th century
**THE VIRGIN AND CHILD.** Oil on panel 53.2×42.4. *Transferred in 1922 from the Stroganov Palace Museum, Petrograd.*

**65. HERRI MET DE BLES.** *C.* 1510 — after 1555
**LANDSCAPE WITH THE FLIGHT INTO EGYPT.** Oil on panel. 33×59.7. *Purchased in 1899 from the Martin Schubart collection, Munich; before that, in the 19th century, in the von Friesen collection, Dresden.*

**66. PIETER BRUEGHEL THE YOUNGER.** *C.* 1564—1638
**ST JOHN PREACHING TO THE MULTITUDE.** 1604. Oil on canvas (transferred from panel). 107.5×167. *Purchased in 1889 from the collection of Baron Pritwitz, St Petersburg.*

**67. FRANS POURBUS THE ELDER.** 1545—1581
**PORTRAIT OF A WOMAN.** Oil on panel. 87✕78. *Purchased in 1764 from the Gotzkowsky collection, Berlin.*

# FLANDERS

Hendrik van Balen
Peter Paul Rubens
Jacob Jordaens
Anthony van Dyck
Frans Snyders

Jan Fyt
David Teniers the Younger
Lodewijck de Vadder

**68. HENDRIK VAN BALEN.** 1575—1632
**ALLEGORY OF VIRTUOUS LIFE.** 1616—17. Oil on panel. 91×122. *Purchased in 1769 from the Brühl collection, Dresden.*

**69. PETER PAUL RUBENS.** 1577—1640
**THE ADORATION OF THE SHEPHERDS.** 1608. Oil on canvas (transferred from panel). 63.5×47 (later additions —
top 5.8, bottom 3.5 — were removed in 1965). *Purchased in 1769 from the Brühl collection, Dresden.*

**70. PETER PAUL RUBENS.** 1577—1640
**HAGAR FLEES ABRAHAM'S HOUSE.** Between 1615 and 1617. Oil on panel. 62.8×76. *Purchased in 1772 from the Crozat collection, Paris.*

**71. PETER PAUL RUBENS.** 1577—1640
**PERSEUS AND ANDROMEDA.** Early 1620s. Oil on canvas (transferred from panel). 99.5×139. *Purchased in 1769 from the Brühl collection, Dresden.*

**72. PETER PAUL RUBENS.** 1577—1640
**CHRIST AT SUPPER WITH SIMON THE PHARISEE.** Late 1610s. Oil on canvas (transferred from panel). 189×254.5.
*Purchased in 1779 from the Walpole collection, Houghton Hall, England; 1681 collection of the Duc de Richelieu, Paris.*

**73, 74. PETER PAUL RUBENS.** 1577—1640
**STATUE OF CERES.** C. 1615. Oil on panel. 90.5×65.5. *Purchased in 1768 from the Cobenzl collection, Brussels.*

**75, 76. PETER PAUL RUBENS.** 1577—1640
**BACCHUS.** Between 1638 and 1640. Oil on canvas (transferred from panel). 191×161.3. *Purchased in 1772 from the Crozat collection, Paris; 1676 collection of the Duc de Richelieu to whom it was sold by the artist's nephew Philip Rubens.*

**77. PETER PAUL RUBENS.** 1577—1640
**MERCURY DEPARTING FROM ANTWERP.** 1634—35. Oil on panel. 76×79. *Purchased in 1779 from the Walpole collection, Houghton Hall, England; 17th century P. H. Lancrinck collection, London.*

**78. PETER PAUL RUBENS.** 1577—1640
**A LION HUNT.** *C.* 1621. Oil on panel. 43×64. *Purchased in 1772 from the Crozat collection, Paris.*

**79. PETER PAUL RUBENS.** 1577—1640
**LANDSCAPE WITH STONE-CARTERS.** *C.* 1620. Oil on canvas (transferred from panel). 86×126.5. *Purchased in 1779 from the Walpole collection, Houghton Hall, England; 1661 Cardinal Mazarin collection, Paris.*

**80. PETER PAUL RUBENS.** 1577—1640
**PORTRAIT OF A LADY IN WAITING TO THE INFANTA ISABELLA (PORTRAIT OF THE ARTIST'S DAUGHTER
CLARA SERENA?).** Between 1623 and 1625. Oil on panel. 64×48. *Purchased in 1772 from the Crozat collection, Paris.*

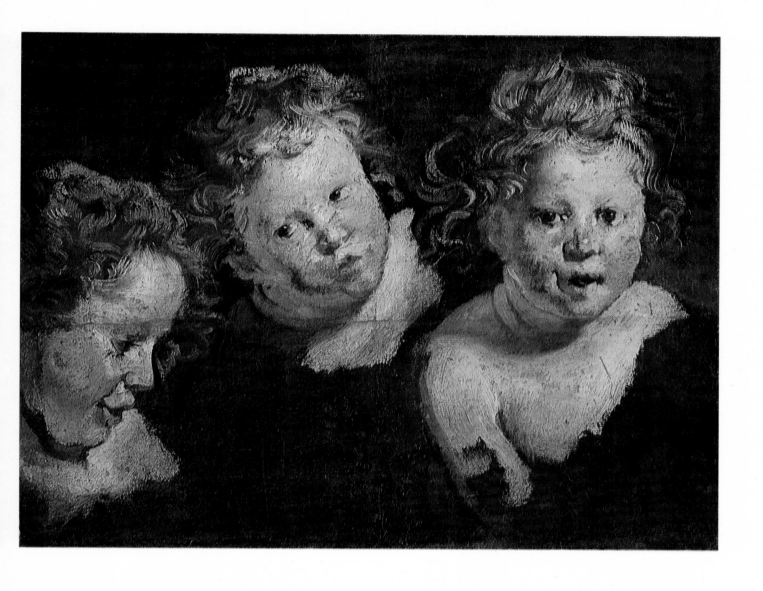

**81. JACOB JORDAENS.** 1593—1678
**THREE STUDIES OF A CHILD'S HEAD.** Between 1618 and 1620. Oil on canvas (transferred from paper glued onto panel).
42.5×53.3. *Acquired between 1763 and 1774.*

**82, 83. JACOB JORDAENS.** 1593—1678
**THE BEAN KING ("THE KING DRINKS!").** *C.* 1638. Oil on canvas (transferred on a new canvas). 157×211. *Transferred in 1922 from the Museum of the Academy of Arts, Petrograd; 19th century Kushelev-Bezborodko collection, St Petersburg.*

**84. ANTHONY VAN DYCK.** 1599—1641
**PORTRAIT OF INIGO JONES.** Early 1630s. Oil on canvas. 64.5✕53.2 (oval within a rectangle). *Purchased in 1779 from the Walpole collection, Houghton Hall, England; before that in the collection of the architect John Webb, England.*

**85. ANTHONY VAN DYCK.** 1599—1641
**SELF-PORTRAIT.** Late 1620s. Oil on canvas. 116.5×93.5 *Purchased in 1772 from the Crozat collection, Paris.*

**86, 87. ANTHONY VAN DYCK.** 1599—1641
**REST ON THE FLIGHT INTO EGYPT (THE VIRGIN WITH PARTRIDGES).** Early 1630s. Oil on canvas. 215× 285.5.
*Purchased in 1779 from the Walpole collection, Houghton Hall, England; 1646—1713 collection of the Princes of Orange,*
*Holland; 1722—33 Falckenburg collection, Rotterdam.*

**88. FRANS SNYDERS.** 1579—1657
**A COOK AT A TABLE WITH DEAD GAME.** Mid-1630s. Oil on canvas. 171✕173. *Purchased in 1764 from the Gotzkowsky collection, Berlin.*

**89. FRANS SNYDERS.** 1579—1657
**FRUIT ON A TABLE.** Oil on panel. 71.6× 103. *Purchased before 1806; transferred in 1934 from the Palace Museum, Pavlovsk, near Leningrad.*

**90. JAN FYT.** 1611—1661
**FRUIT AND A PARROT.** Mid-1640s. Oil on canvas (transferred from panel). 58.3× 90.7. *Bequeathed in 1845 by D. Tatishchev, St Petersburg.*

**91. DAVID TENIERS THE YOUNGER.** 1610—1690
**MONKEYS IN A KITCHEN.** Mid-1640s. Oil on canvas (transferred from panel). 36×50.5. *Purchased in 1815 from the Empress Josephine collection, Malmaison, near Paris.*

**92. DAVID TENIERS THE YOUNGER.** 1610—1690
**VILLAGE FESTIVAL.** 1648. Oil on canvas. 97×138.5 (with a later extension below; without the extension, 9.7×134). *Purchased in 1772 from the Choiseul collection, Paris.*

**93. DAVID TENIERS THE YOUNGER.** 1610—1690
**A VIEW OF THE COUNTRYSIDE NEAR BRUSSELS.** Oil on canvas (transferred from panel). 26.7×38. *Purchased in 1772 from the Crozat collection, Paris.*

**94. LODEWIJCK DE VADDER.** 1605—1655
**FOREST SCENE WITH A RIVER.** Oil on panel. 49✕64. *Acquired in 1915 from the Semionov-Tien-Shansky collection,*
*Petrograd.*

# HOLLAND

Jan van Goyen

Allart van Everdingen

Hans Goderis

Aelbert Cuyp

Jan van der Heyden

Dirk van Delen

Pieter Janssens Elinga

Jan Both

Nicolaes Pietersz Berchem

Adam Pynacker

Johannes Lingelbach

Jacob Isaaksz van Ruisdael

Cornelis Beelt

Gerrit Adriaensz Berckheyde

Pieter Claesz

Balthasar van der Ast

Willem Claesz Heda

Willem Kalf

Job Adriaensz Berckheyde

Jacob Duck

Frans Hals

Jan Steen

Rembrandt

Gabriel Metsu

Pieter de Hooch

Jan Davidsz de Heem

**95. JAN VAN GOYEN.** 1596—1656
**WINTER SCENE NEAR THE HAGUE.** 1645. Oil on panel. 52×70. *Acquired before 1797; it was apparently in Hendrick Verschuring sale, September 17, 1770, The Hague.*

**96. ALLART VAN EVERDINGEN.** 1621—1675
**THE MOUTH OF THE SCHELDE.** Oil on canvas. 62×77.5. *Purchased in 1764 from the Gotzkowsky collection, Berlin.*

**97. HANS GODERIS.** Active 1622—40 in Haarlem
**STORMY SEA.** Late 1620s. Oil on panel. 33×69. *Acquired in 1915 from the Semionov-Tien-Shansky collection, Petrograd.*

**98. AELBERT CUYP.** 1620—1691
**SUNSET ON THE RIVER.** Between 1650 and 1655. Oil on panel. 38.5×53. *Transferred in 1930 from the Palace Museum, Pavlovsk, near Leningrad; entered the Pavlovsk Palace before 1806 probably from the collection of Prince Potiomkin of Tauride, St Petersburg.*

**99. JAN VAN DER HEYDEN.** 1637—1712
**GOUDESTEIN CASTLE.** Late 1660s—early 1670s. Oil on panel (planked). 46× 56.5. The figures are painted by Adriaen van de Velde. *Purchased in 1772 from the Crozat collection, Paris.*

**100. DIRK VAN DELEN.** 1605—1671
**ENTRANCE TO THE PALACE.** 1667 (?). Oil on panel. 57×65. *The figures were presumably painted by Anthonie Palamedesz. Acquired before 1774.*

**101, 102. PIETER JANSSENS ELINGA.** 1623—1682
**ROOM IN A DUTCH HOUSE.** Late 1660s—early 1670s. Oil on canvas. 61.5✕59. *Acquired in 1912 from the Stroganov collection, St Petersburg.*

**103. JAN BOTH.** *C.* 1618—1652
**ITALIAN LANDSCAPE WITH A ROAD.** Between 1645 and 1650. Oil on canvas. 96×136. *Acquired between 1781 and 1797.*

**104. NICOLAES (CLAES) PIETERSZ BERCHEM.** 1620—1683
**REST OF A HUNTING PARTY.** Oil on canvas. 100×148. *Purchased in 1770 from the Tronchin collection, Geneva.*

**105. NICOLAES (CLAES) PIETERSZ BERCHEM.** 1620—1683
**ITALIAN LANDSCAPE WITH A BRIDGE.** 1656. Oil on panel. 44.5×61. *Purchased in 1772 from the Choiseul collection, Paris.*

**106. ADAM PYNACKER.** 1621—1673
**MOUNTAINOUS LANDSCAPE WITH A WATERFALL.** Oil on canvas. 70×60. *Purchased in 1769 from the Brühl collection, Dresden.*

**107. JOHANNES LINGELBACH.** 1622—1674
**LANDSCAPE WITH A HAY CART.** Oil on canvas. 42×51. *Transferred in 1928 from the Stroganov Palace Museum, Leningrad; 19th century Stroganov collection, St Petersburg.*

**108. JACOB ISAAKSZ VAN RUISDAEL (?).** 1628/29—1682
**RIVER IN A FOREST.** Oil on canvas. 65×78.5 (with an extension, 20 cm wide, at the bottom). *Purchased in 1769 from the Brühl collection, Dresden.*

**109, 110. JACOB ISAAKSZ VAN RUISDAEL.** 1628/29—1682
**THE MARSH.** Oil on canvas. 72.5×99. *Acquired between 1763 and 1774.*

**111. CORNELIS BEELT.** Active *c.* 1660 to 1702
**CELEBRATIONS ON THE GROTE MARKT IN HAARLEM.** Oil on canvas. 101×149. *Acquired before 1859; 19th century Gatchina Palace, near St Petersburg; 1926 transferred back to the Hermitage.*

**112. GERRIT ADRIAENSZ BERCKHEYDE.** 1638—1698
**LEAVING FOR A HUNT.** Oil on canvas. 53×62.5. *Acquired before 1774.*

**113. GERRIT ADRIAENSZ BERCKHEYDE.** 1638—1698
**VIEW OF THE CANAL AND CITY HALL IN AMSTERDAM.** Mid-1670s. Oil on canvas. 53×63. *Purchased in 1770 from the Tronchin collection, Geneva.*

**114. PIETER CLAESZ.** 1596/97—1661
**PIPES AND A BRAZIER.** 1636. Oil on panel. 49×63.5. *Transferred in 1921 from the National Museum Reserve; before that in the collection of V. Argutinsky-Dolgorukov, Petrograd.*

**115. BALTHASAR VAN DER AST.** 1593/94—1657
**STILL LIFE WITH FRUIT.** Early 1620s. Oil on panel. 75×104. *Transferred in 1937 from the Customs Office, Leningrad; late 19th century Kaufman collection, St Petersburg.*

**116. WILLEM CLAESZ HEDA.** 1594—1680/82
**BREAKFAST WITH A LOBSTER.** 1648. Oil on canvas. 118×118. *Transferred in 1920 from the National Museum Reserve.*

**118. JOB ADRIAENSZ BERCKHEYDE.** 1630—1693
**VISIT TO A PAINTER'S STUDIO.** 1659. Oil on panel. 49× 36.5. *Purchased in 1769 from the Brühl collection, Dresden.*

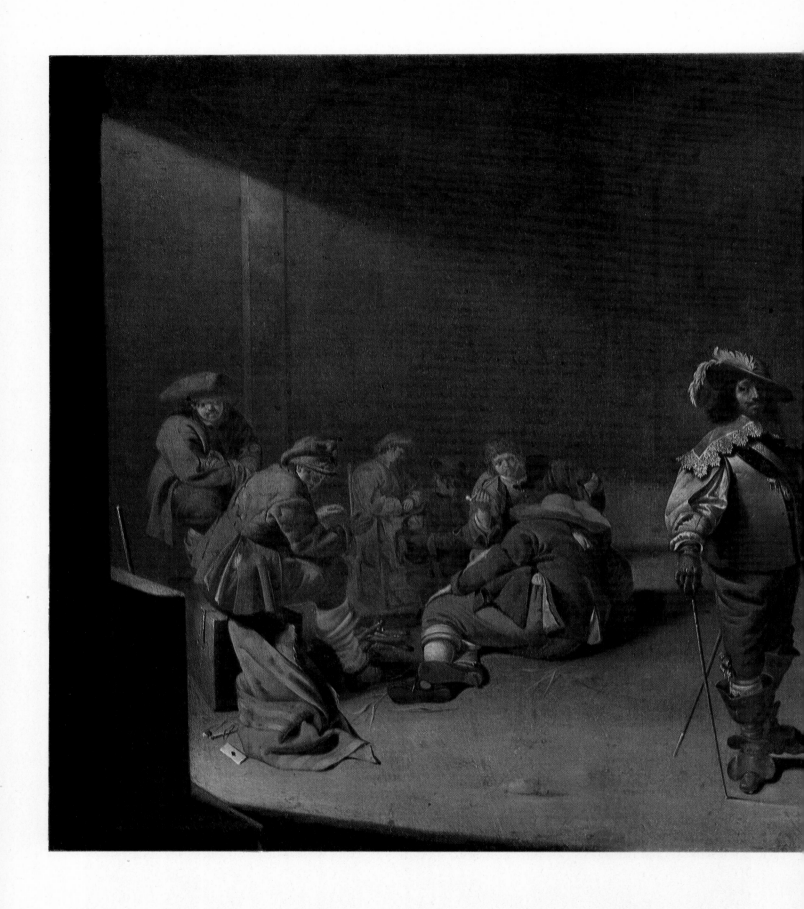

**119. JACOB DUCK.** *C.* 1600 — after 1660
**GUARDROOM.** Oil on canvas (transferred from panel). 37.5 × 70. *Purchased in 1864 from the Fonton collection, St Petersburg.*

**120. FRANS HALS.** 1581/85—1666
**PORTRAIT OF A MAN.** Early 1650s. Oil on canvas. 84.5×67. *Acquired between 1763 and 1774.*

**121. JAN STEEN.** 1625/26—1679
**MARRIAGE CONTRACT.** Late 1640s. Oil on canvas. 65×83. *Purchased in 1717 in Haarlem by Kologrivov on Peter the Great's order; Monplaisir Palace, Peterhof; 1882 transferred to the Hermitage.*

**122. REMBRANDT HARMENSZ VAN RIJN:** 1606—1669
**PORTRAIT OF A YOUNG MAN WITH A LACE COLLAR.** 1634. Oil on panel. 70.5✕52 (oval). *Acquired in 1829*
*from the collection of the Duchess of Saint-Leu, Paris; formerly in the Empress Josephine collection, Malmaison, near Paris.*

**123, 124. REMBRANDT HARMENSZ VAN RIJN.** 1606—1669
**THE HOLY FAMILY WITH ANGELS,** 1645. Oil on canvas, 117×91. *Purchased in 1772 from the Crozat collection, Paris.*

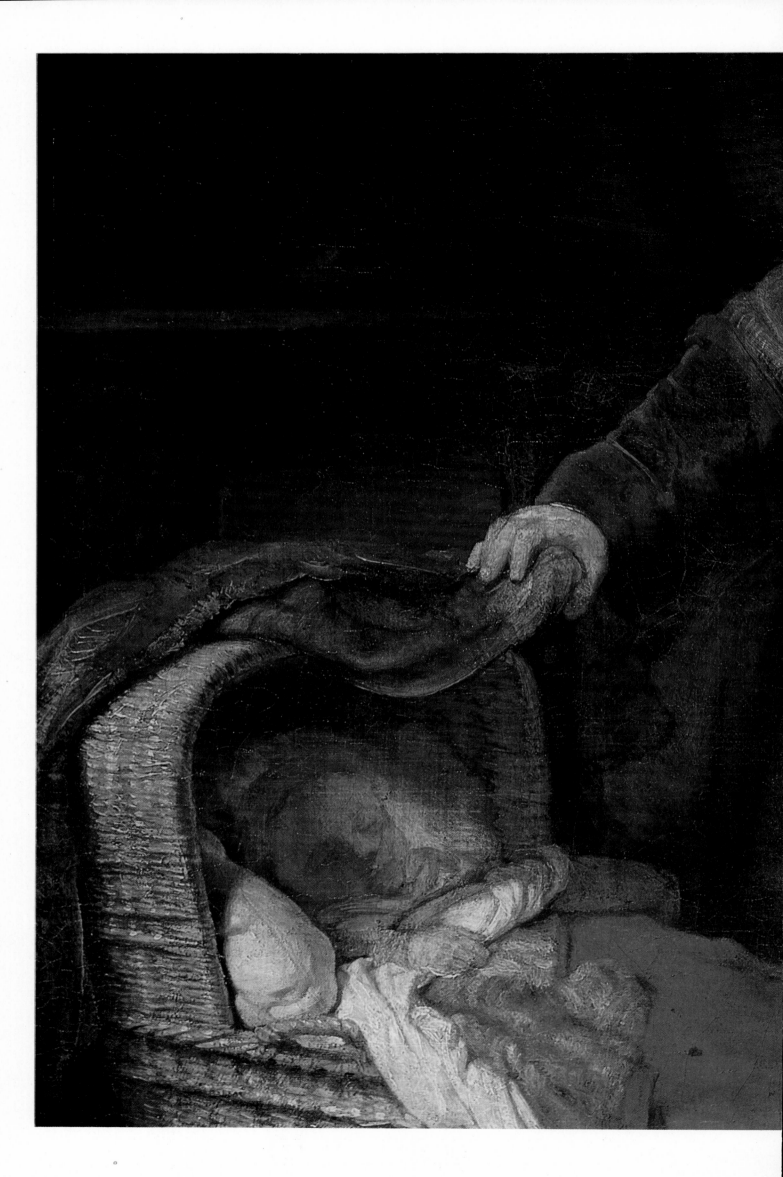

**125, 126. REMBRANDT HARMENSZ VAN RIJN.** 1606—1669
**FLORA.** 1634. Oil on canvas. 125✕101. *Acquired in 1775.*

**127, 128. REMBRANDT HARMENSZ VAN RIJN.** 1606—1669
**DAVID AND JONATHAN.** 1642. Oil on panel. 73×61.5. *Purchased in 1716 for Peter the Great from the collection of Jan Beuningen, Amsterdam; Monplaisir Palace, Peterhof; 1882 transferred to the Hermitage.*

**130. REMBRANDT HARMENSZ VAN RIJN.** 1606—1669
**YOUNG WOMAN WITH EARRINGS.** 1657. Oil on panel. 39.5×32.5. Upper corners enlarged by later additions : left, a triangle with sides measuring 9.7×4.5; right, another one measuring 9.5×4.3. Added later to the lower border, a strip 7.2 cm wide. *Purchased in 1783 from the Baudouin collection, Paris.*

**131. GABRIEL METSU.** 1629—1667
**A SICK LADY AND HER DOCTOR.** 1660s. Oil on canvas. 61×48. *Purchased in 1767 at the de Jullienne sale, Paris.*

**132, 133. GABRIEL METSU.** 1629—1667
**THE PRODIGAL SON.** Oil on canvas (transferred from panel). 77×66. *Purchased in 1770 from the Tronchin collection, Geneva; 1743 Hogenberge collection, Amsterdam; 1754 Lormier collection.*

**134, 135. PIETER DE HOOCH.** 1629 — after 1684

**A WOMAN AND HER MAID.** After 1660. Oil on canvas. 53✕ 42. *Purchased in 1810 from the antiquary La Fontaine, Paris.*

**136.** J AN D AVIDSZ DE H EEM. 1606—1684.
**VASE OF FLOWERS.** Oil on canvas. 87.5×67.5. *Purchased in 1768 from the Cobenzl collection, Brussels.*

# SPAIN

| | |
|---|---|
| Bernat Martorell | Francisco de Zurbarán |
| Juan de Juanes | Antonio Puga |
| Luis de Morales | Diego Velázquez |
| El Greco | Bartolomé Esteban Murillo |
| José de Ribera | Antonio de Pereda |

**137. BERNAT MARTORELL.** Late 14th century — 1452
**ST VINCENT THE MARTYR AND ST VINCENT FERRER.** 1437—52. Oil on panel. 103✕63. *Acquired in 1921 from the National Museum Reserve; formerly in the Ratkov-Rozhnov collection, Petrograd.*

**138. JUAN DE JUANES (JUAN MASIP).** *C.* 1510—1579
**ST VINCENT FERRER.** 1550—55. Oil on canvas (transferred from panel). 143✕ 81. *Acquired in 1815 from the Coeswelt collection, Amsterdam.*

**139. JUAN DE JUANES (JUAN MASIP).** *C.* 1510—1579
**THE ANNUNCIATION TO ST ANNE.** 1550—55. Oil on canvas (transferred from panel). 144.5 × 82.7. *Acquired in 1814 from the Coeswelt collection, Amsterdam.*

**140. LUIS DE MORALES.** *C.* 1509—1586
**MADONNA AND CHILD WITH A CROSS-SHAPED DISTAFF.** 1570s. Oil on canvas (transferred from panel). 71.5×52.
*Bequeathed by D. Tatishchev in 1846.*

**141. EL GRECO (DOMENIKOS THEOTOKOPOULOS).** 1541—1614
**THE APOSTLES PETER AND PAUL.** 1587—92. Oil on canvas. 121.5×105. *Donated by P. Durnovo in 1911.*

**142. JOSÉ DE RIBERA.** 1591—1652
**AN ALLEGORY OF HISTORY.** 1616—20. Oil on canvas. 113×81. *Acquired in 1920 from the National Museum Reserve; formerly in the Wolfsohn collection, Petrograd.*

**143. JOSÉ DE RIBERA.** 1591—1652
**ST SEBASTIAN AND ST IRENE.** 1628. Oil on canvas. 156×188. *Purchased in 1829 from the collection of the Duchess of Saint-Leu; formerly in the Empress Josephine collection, Malmaison, near Paris (since 1811 Malmaison Gallery).*

**144, 145. FRANCISCO DE ZURBARÁN.** 1598—1664
**ST LAWRENCE.** 1636. Oil on canvas. 292✕225. *Purchased in 1852 from the Soult collection, Paris; formerly in the church of the Monastery of San José (La Merced Descalzas), Seville; then in the Alcázar, Seville.*

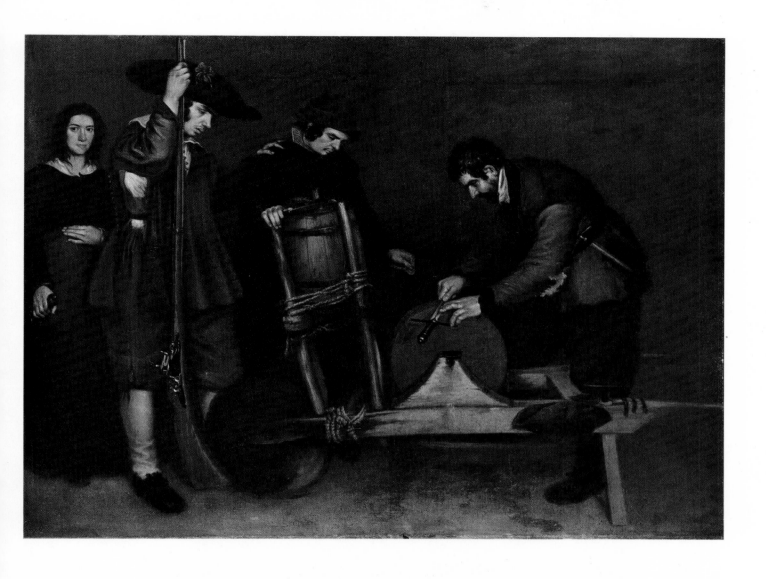

146. **FRANCISCO DE ZURBARÁN.** 1598—1664
**ST FERDINAND.** 1630—35. Oil on canvas. 129×61. *Acquired in 1922; formerly in the Monastery of San José (La Merced Descalzas), Seville (?); 1810—52 Soult collection, Paris; S. Panina collection, Petrograd.*

147. **ANTONIO PUGA.** 1602—1648
**THE GRINDER.** 1630s. Oil on canvas. 120×160. *Acquired in 1815 from the Coeswelt collection, Amsterdam.*

**148. DIEGO RODRÍGUEZ DE SILVA Y VELÁZQUEZ.** 1599—1660
**LUNCHEON.** *C.* 1617. Oil on canvas. 108.5×102. *Acquired before 1774; until 1895 in the Tauride Palace and in the Hermitage storerooms, St Petersburg.*

**149. DIEGO RODRÍGUEZ DE SILVA Y VELÁZQUEZ.** 1599—1660
**COUNT-DUKE OF OLIVARES.** *C.* 1638. Oil on canvas. 67×54.5. *Acquired in 1814 from the Coeswelt collection, Amsterdam.*

**150. BARTOLOMÉ ESTEBAN MURILLO.** 1617—1682
THE ANNUNCIATION. 1655—60. Oil on canvas. 142×107.5. *Acquired in 1814 from the Coeswelt collection, Amsterdam.*

**151. BARTOLOMÉ ESTEBAN MURILLO.** 1617—1682
**THE ADORATION OF THE SHEPHERDS.** 1646—50. Oil on canvas. 197×147. *Purchased in 1779 from the Walpole collection, Houghton Hall, England.*

**152. B**ARTOLOMÉ **E**STEBAN **M**URILLO. 1617—1682
**THE HOLY FAMILY.** 1660—65. Oil on panel. 23.8×18. *Purchased in 1772 from the Crozat collection, Paris; until*
*1756 Tallard collection, Besançon.*

**153. BARTOLOMÉ ESTEBAN MURILLO.** 1617—1682
**THE LIBERATION OF ST PETER.** *C.* 1667. Oil on canvas. 124×115. *Purchased in 1852 from the Soult collection, Paris; 1667 Hospital de la Caridad, Seville; 1810 Alcázar, Seville.*

**154, 155. BARTOLOMÉ ESTEBAN MURILLO.** 1617—1682
**THE INFANT JESUS AND ST JOHN.** 1655—60. Oil on canvas. 124×115. *Purchased in 1852 from the Soult collection, Paris.*

**156. ANTONIO DE PEREDA.** 1602—1678
**STILL LIFE WITH A CABINET.** 1652. Oil on canvas. 80✕94. *Acquired in 1815 from the Coeswelt collection, Amsterdam.*

# GERMANY

Lucas Cranach the Elder
Bartholomaeus Bruyn the Elder
Georg Flegel
Ambrosius Holbein
Hans Wertinger
Hendrick van der Borcht
Christopher Paudiss

Johann Heinrich Schönfeld
Johann Rottenhammer
Anton Raphael Mengs
Johann Heinrich Wilhelm Tischbein
Jacob Philipp Hackert
Angelica Kauffmann

# AUSTRIA

Friedrich Heinrich Füger
Johann Georg Platzer

PELLE · CVPIDINEOS · TOTO ⟶ CONAMINE · LVXVS
NE · TVA · POSSIDEAT ⟶ PECTORA · CECA · VENVS

**157. LUCAS CRANACH THE ELDER.** 1472—1553
**VENUS AND CUPID.** 1509. Oil on canvas (transferred from panel). 213×102. *Purchased in 1769 from the Brühl collection, Dresden.*

**158. LUCAS CRANACH THE ELDER.** 1472—1553
THE VIRGIN AND CHILD UNDER THE APPLE TREE. Oil on canvas (transferred from panel). 87✕59. *Acquired in 1851.*

**159. LUCAS CRANACH THE ELDER.** 1472—1553
**PORTRAIT OF A WOMAN.** 1526. Oil on panel. 88.5×58.5. *Acquired before 1797.*

**160. LUCAS CRANACH THE ELDER.** 1472—1553
**PORTRAIT OF CARDINAL ALBRECHT OF BRANDENBURG.** 1526. Oil on canvas (transferred from panel). 40×24.5.
*Acquired before 1797.*

**161. BARTHOLOMAEUS (BARTHEL) BRUYN THE ELDER.** C. 1493—1555
**PORTRAIT OF A MAN AND HIS THREE SONS.** Late 1530s—early 1540s. Oil on canvas (transferred from panel).
75.5×46. *Purchased in 1768 from the Cobenzl collection, Brussels.*

**163. AMBROSIUS HOLBEIN.** *C.* 1495— *c.* 1520
**PORTRAIT OF A YOUNG MAN.** 1518. Tempera and oil on panel. 44×32.5. *Acquired around 1773.*

**164. HANS WERTINGER,** called **THE SWABIAN.** 1465/70—1533
**VILLAGE FESTIVAL (OCTOBER).** 1525—30. Oil on panel. 22.5×40. *Transferred in 1925 from the Shuvalov Palace Museum, Leningrad.*

**165. HENDRICK VAN DER BORCHT.** 1583—1660
**STILL LIFE WITH ANTIQUITIES.** Oil on copper. Diameter 34.5 (tondo). *Purchased in 1889 from the V. Belevich
collection, St Petersburg.*

**166. CHRISTOPHER PAUDISS.** C. 1625—1666
**STILL LIFE.** 1660. Oil on canvas (transferred from panel). 62×46.5. *Acquired before 1859.*

**167. JOHANN HEINRICH SCHÖNFELD.** 1609—1684
**RAPE OF THE SABINE WOMEN.** Oil on canvas. 98.5×134. *Acquired in the second half of the 18th century; Gatchina Palace, near St Petersburg; 1926 transferred back to the Hermitage.*

**168. JOHANN (HANS) ROTTENHAMMER.** 1564—1624
**THE BANQUET OF THE GODS (MARRIAGE OF PELEUS AND THETIS).** 1600. Oil on copper. 34×45. *Purchased in 1769 with the Brühl collection, Dresden.*

**169. ANTON RAPHAEL MENGS.** 1728—1779
**PERSEUS AND ANDROMEDA.** 1770s. Oil on canvas. 227×153.5. *Acquired in 1780. According to old written sources, the picture was commissioned by an Englishman, Sir Watkin William Winn, who paid Mengs 300 livres. In 1778, the painting was sent to Britain by sea, but the ship was captured by French pirates who sold the picture in Cádiz. It was bought by the French Minister of the Maritime Affairs de Sartine. In 1779, Grimm and the Foreign Secretary of France de Verjin negotiated the purchase of this painting for Catherine II of Russia. It was first brought to Versailles and then, in 1780, to St Petersburg.*

**170. ANTON RAPHAEL MENGS.** 1728—1779
**SELF-PORTRAIT.** *C.* 1775. Oil on panel (planked). 102×77. *Acquired around 1794 (at first was housed at the Pavlovsk Palace, near St Petersburg).*

**171. FRIEDRICH HEINRICH FÜGER.** 1751—1818
**PORTRAIT OF PRINCE NIKOLAI YUSUPOV.** 1783 (?). Oil on canvas. 112✕ 87. *Transferred in 1925 from the Yusupov Palace Museum, Leningrad.*

**172. JOHANN HENRICH WILHELM TISCHBEIN (GOETHE-TISCHBEIN).** 1751—1829
CONRADIN OF SWABIA AND FRIEDRICH OF BADEN AWAITING THE VERDICT. 1785. Oil on canvas. 65.5×91.5.
*Acquired in 1784; 19th century Gatchina Palace, near St Petersburg; 1931 transferred back to the Hermitage.*

**173. JACOB PHILIPP HACKERT.** 1737—1807
LANDSCAPE WITH A SCENE OF AN ANTIQUE FESTIVAL. 1781. Oil on canvas. 66×89.5. *Transferred in 1925 from the Yusupov Palace Museum, Leningrad.*

**174. ANGELICA KAUFFMANN.** 1741—1807
PARTING OF ABELARD AND ELOISA. Before 1780s. Oil on canvas. Diameter 65.5 (tondo in a square). *Acquired before 1797.*

**175. JOHANN GEORG PLATZER.** 1704—1761
CLEOPATRA'S BANQUET. Oil on copper. 76×58. *Acquired before 1774.*

# ENGLAND

William Dobson          Godfrey Kneller
Michael Dahl            George Romney
John Wootton            John Hoppner
Thomas Gainsborough     Joshua Reynolds
George Morland
Joseph Wright

**176.  WILLIAM DOBSON.** 1611—1646
**PORTRAIT OF ABRAHAM VAN DER DOORT.** C. 1640. Oil on canvas. 45×38. *Purchased in 1779 from the Walpole collection, Houghton Hall, England; before that in the Richardson collection, London.*

**178. JOHN WOOTTON.** 1682—1764
**HOUNDS AND A MAGPIE.** Before 1752. Oil on canvas. 152×128. *Purchased in 1779 from the Walpole collection, Houghton Hall, England.*

**181. GEORGE MORLAND.** 1763—1804
**APPROACHING STORM.** 1791. Oil on canvas. 85×117. *Acquired in 1919 from the Ferzen collection, Petrograd.*

**182. JOSEPH WRIGHT OF DERBY.** 1734—1797
**THE ANNUAL GIRANDOLA. CASTEL SANT'ANGELO.** Between 1774 and 1778. Oil on canvas. 162.5× 213. *Purchased in 1779 from the artist.*

**183. GODFREY KNELLER.** 1646(49?)—1723
**PORTRAIT OF JOHN LOCKE.** 1697. Oil on canvas. 76×64 (oval within a rectangle). *Purchased in 1779 from the Walpole collection, Houghton Hall, England.*

**184. George Romney.** 1734—1802
**PORTRAIT OF MRS HARRIET GREER.** 1781. Oil on canvas. 76×64. *Bequeathed by A. Khitrovo in 1912.*

**185. JOHN HOPPNER.** 1758—1810
**PORTRAIT OF RICHARD BRINSLEY SHERIDAN (?).** Oil on canvas. 77×64. *Bequeathed by A. Khitrovo in 1912.*

**186, 187. JOSHUA REYNOLDS.** 1723—1792
**THE INFANT HERCULES STRANGLING THE SERPENTS.** 1788. Oil on canvas. 303✕297. *Purchased in 1789 from the artist.*

**188. JOSHUA REYNOLDS.** 1723—1792
**CUPID UNTYING THE GIRDLE OF VENUS.** 1788. Oil on canvas. 127.5×101. *Acquired in 1792 from the collection of Prince Potiomkin of Tauride, St Petersburg. This picture was commissioned to Reynolds for Prince Potiomkin by Lord Carysfort in 1788.*

# FRANCE

Master of the Thuison Altarpiece
Master of St Sebastian
Corneille de Lyon
Anonymous French painter
of the 16th century
Jacques Bellange
Le Valentin
Simon Vouet
Louis Le Nain
Nicolas Poussin
Jean Lemaire
Claude Lorrain
Pierre (?) Montallier
Antoine Watteau
Jean-Baptiste Pater
Nicolas Lancret
Jacob-Ferdinand Voet (?)
Jean-Baptiste Santerre
Jean-Baptiste Monnoyer

Nicolas de Largillière
Joseph Vivien
François Desportes
Jean-Baptiste Oudry
Alexis Grimou
François Boucher
Jean-Baptiste Siméon Chardin
Jean-Baptiste Perronneau
Carle Vanloo
Jean-Baptiste Greuze
Jean-Honoré Fragonard
Claude Joseph Vernet
Hubert Robert
Louise-Elisabeth Vigée-Lebrun

**189, 190. MASTER OF THE THUISON ALTARPIECE.** Active 15th century
**THE TRIUMPHAL ENTRY INTO JERUSALEM.** *C.* 1470. Oil on panel. 116.5×51.5. *Purchased in 1919 from the collection of A. Gagarin, Petrograd.*

**191, 192. MASTER OF ST SEBASTIAN (JOSSE LIEFERINXE?).** Active late 15th century
**ST SEBASTIAN BEFORE EMPERORS DIOCLETIAN AND MAXIMIAN.** Oil on panel. 81.5×55.7. *Acquired in 1931 from the "Antiquariat"; 19th century Volkonskaya collection, St Petersburg.*

**193. CORNEILLE DE LYON.** Early 16th century — 1575
**PORTRAIT OF A LADY.** Oil on panel. 20.5 × 15.7. *Transferred in 1925 from the Shuvalov Palace Museum, Leningrad; before that in the Shuvalov collection, St Petersburg.*

**194. ANONYMOUS FRENCH PAINTER.** Active 16th century
**PORTRAIT OF HENRI, DUKE OF ANJOU (?).** Between 1560 and 1570. Oil on panel. 47.8 × 34.2. *Purchased in 1772 from the Crozat collection, Paris.*

---

**195. JACQUES BELLANGE.** Active 1602—17
**THE MOURNING OF CHRIST.** *C.* 1616. Oil on canvas. 116.3×173. *Acquired in 1967 through the State Purchasing Commission; 1925 Khanukyan collection, Moscow.*

---

**196. LE VALENTIN (JEAN DE BOULOGNE).** 1594—1632
**CHRIST DRIVING THE MONEY-CHANGERS FROM THE TEMPLE.** *C.* 1632. Oil on canvas. 192×266.5. *Purchased in 1772 from the Crozat collection, Paris.*

---

**197. SIMON VOUET.** 1590—1649
**PORTRAIT OF ANNE OF AUSTRIA AS MINERVA.** After 1643. Oil on canvas. 202×172. *Acquired in 1931 from the "Antiquariat".*

**198. LOUIS LE NAIN.** 1600/10—1648
**A MILKWOMAN'S FAMILY.** C. 1641. Oil on canvas. 51×59. *Acquired between 1763 and 1774.*

**199. LOUIS LE NAIN.** 1600/10—1648
**VISIT TO GRANDMOTHER.** Oil on canvas. 58.6×73. *Purchased in 1772 from the Crozat collection, Paris.*

**200. NICOLAS POUSSIN.** 1594—1665

**VENUS, FAUN AND PUTTI.** Oil on canvas. 71.7×56. *Purchased in 1822 from the Korsakov collection; formerly in the Crozat collection, Paris. On the reverse there is the seal of François Tronchin with which he probably marked the pictures selected from this collection for Catherine II. Evidently, Catherine II presented the painting to one of her retinue, from whom Korsakov received it in his turn.*

**201. NICOLAS POUSSIN.** 1594—1665
**TANCRED AND ERMINIA.** *C.* 1631. Oil on canvas. 98.2× 146.7. *Purchased in 1766 from the Aved collection, Paris.*

**202. JEAN LEMAIRE,** called **LEMAIRE-POUSSIN (?).** 1597—1659
**LANDSCAPE WITH SARCOPHAGUS.** Late 1640s — early 1650s. Oil on canvas. 98.5×133. *Purchased in 1783 from the Baudouin collection, Paris, as a work of Nicolas Poussin; since mid-19th century Gatchina Palace, near St Petersburg; 1926 transferred back to the Hermitage.*

**203. CLAUDE GELLÉE,** called **LORRAIN.** 1600—1682
**LANDSCAPE WITH JACOB, RACHEL AND LEAH BY THE WELL (MORNING).** 1666. Oil on canvas. 113×157. *Purchased in 1815 from the Empress Josephine collection, Malmaison, near Paris.*

**204. CLAUDE GELLÉE,** called **LORRAIN.** 1600—1682
**LANDSCAPE WITH JACOB WRESTLING WITH THE ANGEL (NIGHT).** 1672. Oil on canvas. 113×157. *Purchased in 1815 from the Empress Josephine collection, Malmaison, near Paris.*

**205. P**IERRE **(?) M**ONTALLIER. *C.* 1643—1697
**DEEDS OF CHARITY.** Mid-1660s. Oil on canvas. 44.6×53.4. *Acquired between 1783 and 1797; 1809 Hermitage Pavilion, Peterhof; 1921 transferred back to the Hermitage.*

**206. ANTOINE WATTEAU.** 1684—1721
**SAVOYARD WITH A MARMOT.** Oil on canvas. 40.5×32.5. *Acquired before 1774 (until 1734 belonged to Watteau's teacher Claude Audran).*

**207, 208. Antoine Watteau.** 1684—1721

**ACTORS OF THE COMÉDIE-FRANÇAISE.** Oil on panel. 20×25. *Purchased in 1772 from the Crozat collection, Paris; since mid-19th century Gatchina Palace, near St Petersburg; 1920 transferred back to the Hermitage.*

**209. JEAN-BAPTISTE PATER.** 1695—1736
**SCENE IN A PARK** (right-hand wing of a triptych). Oil on canvas. 149×84. *Acquired between 1773 and 1785; presented by Catherine II to Count Orlov; 19th and the early 20th centuries Marble Palace, St Petersburg, from where the central panel was transferred to the Hermitage in 1920 and the side wings to the Museum of Fine Arts, Moscow in 1921; since 1934 the entire triptych is in the Hermitage.*

**210, 211. NICOLAS LANCRET.** 1690—1743
**LA CAMARGO.** 1732. Oil on canvas. 45×55. *Acquired before 1774; 1902 transferred from the Winter Palace to the Hermitage.*

**212. Jacob-Ferdinand Voet** (?). 1635—1700 (?)
**PORTRAIT OF HORTENSE MANCINI** (?). Oil on canvas. 80.3×65.5 (oval). *Transferred in 1923 from the National Museum Reserve; before that in the Oliv collection, Petrograd.*

**213. JEAN-BAPTISTE SANTERRE.** 1651—1717
**PORTRAIT OF TWO ACTRESSES.** 1699. Oil on canvas. 146×114. *Acquired in 1766; since mid-19th century Gatchina Palace, near St Petersburg; 1926 transferred back to the Hermitage.*

**214. JEAN-BAPTISTE MONNOYER.** 1634—1699
**FLOWERS AND FRUIT.** Oil on canvas. 74.5× 121.5. *Acquired in 1933 through the State Purchasing Commission.*

**215. NICOLAS DE LARGILLIÈRE.** 1656—1746
**ECHEVINS OF THE CITY OF PARIS DISCUSSING THE CELEBRATIONS AND DINNER AT THE TOWN HALL ON THE OCCASION OF LOUIS XIV's RECOVERY AFTER ILLNESS IN 1687.** Oil on canvas. 68× 101. *Purchased in 1772 from the Crozat collection, Paris.*

**216. JOSEPH VIVIEN.** 1657—1734
**PORTRAIT OF THE ARCHITECT JULES HARDOUIN-MANSART.** Between 1693 and 1699. Oil on canvas. 74× 59 (oval). *Acquired in 1922; formerly in the Miatlev collection, Petrograd.*

**217. FRANÇOIS DESPORTES.** 1661—1743
**STILL LIFE WITH DEAD GAME AND VEGETABLES.** Before 1730. Oil on canvas. 121×135. *Purchased in 1769 from the Brühl collection, Dresden; 1918 transferred from the Winter Palace to the Hermitage.*

**218. JEAN-BAPTISTE OUDRY.** 1686—1755
**A DOG POINTING A PARTRIDGE.** 1725. Oil on canvas. 129×162. *Purchased in 1764 from the Gotzkowsky collection, Berlin; 19th century Gatchina Palace, near St Petersburg; 1925 transferred back to the Hermitage.*

**219. ALEXIS GRIMOU.** 1678—1733
**A YOUNG LADY IN A THEATRICAL COSTUME.** 1730s. Oil on canvas. 74× 59. *Acquired between 1763 and 1774;*
*19th century Hermitage Pavilion, Peterhof; 1905 transferred back to the Hermitage.*

**220. FRANÇOIS BOUCHER.** 1703—1770
**LANDSCAPE NEAR BEAUVAIS.** Early 1740s. Oil on canvas. 49×58. *Acquired in 1923 from the Oliv collection, Petrograd.*

**221. JEAN-BAPTISTE SIMÉON CHARDIN.** 1699—1779
**STILL LIFE WITH ATTRIBUTES OF THE ARTS.** 1766. Oil on canvas. 112× 140.5. *Purchased in 1766 from the artist;*
*1854 sold on Nicholas I's orders; van der Pal collection, near Oranienbaum; 1926 returned to the Hermitage.*

**222. JEAN-BAPTISTE PERRONNEAU.** 1715—1783
**A BOY WITH A BOOK.** 1745—46. Oil on canvas. 63×52. *Purchased in 1781 from the A. Teplov collection, St Petersburg;*
*formerly in the G. Teplov collection, Oriol Province.*

**223. CARLE VANLOO.** 1705—1765
**SPANISH CONCERT (CONVERSATION ESPAGNOLE).** 1754. Oil on canvas. 164× 129. *Purchased in 1772 from the Geoffrin collection, Paris; 1899 transferred from the Winter Palace to the Hermitage.*

**224. JEAN-BAPTIST GREUZE.** 1725—1805
**A SPOILT CHILD.** Early 1760s. Oil on canvas. 66.5× 56. *Purchased in 1923 from the collection of Paskevich, Petrograd; 18th century A. Bezborodko collection, St Petersburg.*

**225. JEAN-HONORÉ FRAGONARD.** 1732—1806
**THE STOLEN KISS.** Late 1780s. Oil on canvas. 45×55. *Acquired in 1895 from the Lazienki Palace, Warsaw; before that in the collection of Stanislaus Augustus of Poland.*

**226, 227. JEAN-HONORÉ FRAGONARD.** 1732—1806
**THE LOST FORFEIT.** Oil on canvas. 47× 60. *Transferred in 1925 from the Yusupov Palace Museum, Leningrad.*

**228. CLAUDE JOSEPH VERNET.** 1714—1789
**VIEW IN THE PARK OF VILLA LODOVISI IN ROME.** 1749. Oil on canvas. 74.5× 99.5. *Transferred in 1922 from the Museum of the Academy of Arts, Petrograd; 1768 presented to the Academy by Catherine II; before that in the La Villette collection.*

**229. HUBERT ROBERT.** 1733—1808
**ARCHITECTURAL VIEW WITH A CANAL.** 1783. Oil on canvas. 129× 182.5. *Transferred in 1886 from the Golitsyn Museum, Moscow; 18th century Choiseul-Goufier collection, Paris; 1912 transferred to the Hermitage from the Winter Palace, St Petersburg.*

**230. HUBERT ROBERT.** 1733—1808
**LAUNDRESSES IN THE RUINS.** Early 1760s. Oil on canvas. 72× 88. *Transferred in 1926 from the Stroganov Palace Museum, Leningrad.*

**231. L<small>OUISE</small>-E<small>LISABETH</small> V<small>IGÉE</small>-L<small>EBRUN</small>.** 1755—1842
**PORTRAIT OF PRINCE ALEXANDER KURAKIN.** 1797. Oil on canvas. 96 × 76. *Acquired in 1923 from the Oliv
collection, Petrograd; 19th century Kurakin collection, Moscow.*

# INDEX

Numbers refer to plates

# ЭРМИТАЖ
## Западноевропейская живопись XIII—XVIII веков

Альбом (на английском языке)
Издательство „Аврора“. Санкт-Петербург. 1993
Изд. № 2681
ГПП им. Ивана Федорова.
Printed and bound in Russia